Leading Lean by Living Lean

In this book, Philip Holt details and explains what is probably the most important part of becoming a Lean leader – living and practicing what you preach. To do this you must believe in what you're doing, understand what it means and what you need to do, and do it every day. The author, through his engineering background, has fully embraced the Plan, Do, Check, Act (PDCA) model of Deming / Shewhart but has adapted David Bovis' Believe, Think, Feel, Act (BTFA) model to understand why logic and facts are very often not the principal players in the game of change. In Leading Lean by Living Lean, the author describes how you can take both the PDCA and BTFA models into account and has sectioned the book into three prime parts: 1. Head: How you learn and understand the Lean principles and their application. 2. Hands: How you practice Lean Leadership daily. 3. Heart: How you internalize and believe in Lean Leadership. Through this book, you, the Lean practitioner, whether aspiring or experienced, will have everything that you need to "lead it," "do it," and "live it." The nature of this book is more "why to" than "how to" – the author knows that he cannot tell you how to lead, do, or live Lean; he can only explain why it is so important and share his knowledge, experiences, failures, and successes. This book isn't so much a self-help book as a self-reflection book and it can point you in the proper direction, but… the book won't change you; only you can change you! Essentially, with this book, the author wants those who think of Lean as a toolkit, who believe that Lean can be project managed, or who argue about Lean versus Six Sigma and misunderstand the fundamental depth of impact that true Lean Leadership has on an organization, to be disabused of any or all of those notions. This book is aimed at those leaders who seek to experience the full transformative effects of Lean in their organizations and want to practice it at the principle level of deployment. Holt's aim is to help business leaders enhance who they are by changing what they do and the way that they do it.

Leading Lean by Living Lean

Changing How You Lead, Not Who You Are

Philip Holt

Routledge
Taylor & Francis Group

A PRODUCTIVITY PRESS BOOK

First published 2022
by Routledge
605 Third Avenue, New York, NY 10158

and by Routledge
4 Park Square, Milton Park, Abingdon, Oxon, OX14 4RN

Routledge is an imprint of the Taylor & Francis Group, an informa business

Library of Congress Cataloging-in-Publication Data
A catalog record for this title has been requested

ISBN: 978-1-032-17007-7 (hbk)
ISBN: 978-1-032-17005-3 (pbk)
ISBN: 978-1-003-25138-5 (ebk)

DOI: 10.4324/9781003251385

Typeset in Garamond
by Newgen Publishing UK

Contents

Foreword by Jon Tudor

For the past two decades, I've worked with hundreds of Lean practitioners and experts and, in doing so, discovered the 'Lean paradox': Why do so many Lean practitioners, who coach and train people in Lean, fail to apply Lean thinking in their own work and lives?

Leading Lean by Living Lean is for the Lean practitioner, aspiring or experienced, who really wants to change the way that they work and become highly effective by applying Lean thinking in their own daily life. While there are many books written on Lean leadership, this book is a definitive work on the discipline of *Living Lean* inwardly.

I am excited about this book as it emphasises the importance and significance of the Lean practitioner becoming the Lean 'role-model' within their organisation. To truly get the most out of this book you must be a practitioner who is committed to the process of change that will help you to develop into the Lean role-model in your organisation.

Philip provides his personal reflections from over 30 years of Lean transformation triumphs and failures but essentially this book is about you and how you can personally change and live Lean in your daily life.

My own Lean journey has involved travelling the world, studying and benchmarking hundreds of sites, most of which are struggling to embed and sustain a Lean thinking culture. Through adopting many of the lessons and insights in this book you, the Lean practitioner, can become the Lean role-model, which will become a major enabler of the work that you are doing in Lean, and have a significant impact on the leaders and colleagues that you are working with.

Like Philip, I've had the benefit of working with and being influenced by some of the best Lean minds of the past 30 years. I first met Philip whilst I was at The Manufacturing Institute, a privileged role in which I met and worked with some of the thought leaders of the Lean philosophy: Dr Richard Schonberger, the man who coined the phrase 'world class manufacturing' in the 1980s; Stephen Spear, Harvard professor and author of 'Decoding the DNA of the Toyota Production System'; Professor Dan Jones, co-author of *The Machine That Changed the World*; and the UK's leading Lean authority (although born and raised in South Africa), Professor John Bicheno from the Lean Enterprise Research Council (LERC).

After moving to the *Lean Management Journal*, interviewing and sharing best practice from other leading Lean figureheads like Jim Womack and John Shook from the Lean Enterprise Institute, I first started working with the author, and it was a surprisingly hot, summer day in Manchester in 2010 when Philip shared his insights as a Lean practitioner at the Journal's Lean Directors Masterclass. Two key components of his experience on display were how Lean itself is a management philosophy, not a series of tools, and that leadership is key to a successful Lean transformation. These insights and best practice thinking made their way into his first two books, *Leading with Lean* and *The Simplicity of Lean*.

I received the original manuscript for this, his third book, in May 2020 and at the start of the Covid-19 global pandemic, a time of immense change for everyone's personal and working life. Having read and provided my feedback on the book, I continued with the reality of working from home in a time of rapid change.

However, upon reviewing the next revision of the manuscript in August I realised that something truly unexpected had happened in my own Lean journey. Whilst reading the manuscript for the second time, I realised what a profound effect reading the book had had on my own way of working. Almost subconsciously I began to understand that I had been applying Lean thinking in my own daily work and I began reflecting on the changes that I needed to make in my own business, and with this I engaged in deep self-reflection and began using many of the approaches set out in this book.

I had been using an element of leader standard work in the past, but I now focussed it into something that I actively used on a daily basis. Applying short interval controls in my own work proved a game changer, as it highlighted how off-course on delivering on my own daily plans I had been. I started to break my work down and use many of the techniques and found myself improving my own personal effectiveness. Reviewing this book couldn't have happened at a better time and it helped me to pull together my existing Lean knowledge, think about the 'Why', and apply it to my own life.

I do urge you to get your pen out when reading this book and complete the Hansei at the end of each chapter. Philip has always understood the importance of deep self-reflection in his career, and as a Lean practitioner I do hope that you can develop this lifelong approach to self-development and become the Lean role-model in your organisation.

I hope in the pages of this book you'll be able to learn from Philip and enjoy his insight and best practice know-how as much as I have, and that your own Lean journey is a transformational one.

Jon Tudor
Founder and Director, True North Excellence
Fellow, Business School, Manchester Metropolitan University

Jon Tudor is a Lean explorer and educationist. He studied Business at Manchester Metropolitan University and received a Post-Graduate Certificate of Education at the University of Manchester. He has been responsible for running Lean events and training programmes for The Manufacturing Institute and the UK's Manufacturing Advisory Service. He administered and launched the Shingo Prize for Operational Excellence in the UK and Ireland. His 20 years involved in promoting Lean best practice include: Head of Events for *The Manufacturer* magazine; Editor of the *Lean Management Journal*; former UK Region President for the Association for Manufacturing Excellence (AME); and Advisory Board Member for the Society of Operational Excellence. With True North Excellence he is focused on supporting organisations on their Lean transformation journey, applying the latest best practice approaches to creating a Lean culture.

Preface

Lean is probably one of the most misunderstood leadership concepts in business, and many people would even question why I would refer to it as a leadership concept. Surely it's a manufacturing methodology, hence why it's often referred to as Lean Manufacturing and is the descendent of the Toyota Production System (TPS). However, this is precisely why books like *Leading Lean by Living Lean*, over 30 years after *The Machine That Changed the World*[1] was first published, are so necessary.

Somehow, despite the many practitioners, academics and consultants who collectively have sought to understand, codify and teach the lessons and best practices of Lean Leadership, in my experience the majority of people still have a woefully inadequate comprehension of what it really means to live, practise and succeed with Lean, spending an inordinate amount of time running tool-based, point improvement activities, and completely missing the holistic cultural transformation necessary for an organisation to be able to emulate the truly Lean enterprises.

Leading Lean by Living Lean is my third book and the last that I will write in terms of 'why to' think, lead and live Lean. I believe that with this final tome I've completed the triumvirate of books that, together, provide the reader with everything that they need to make Lean Transformation a reality in their organisation and to get past the paradigm of Lean as a manufacturing or tool-based system and, instead, appreciate and practise it as the People-based cultural phenomenon that it truly is.

In my first book, *Leading with Lean*, I went into the detail of how to lead a Lean transformation in any organization, using the VIRAL model as the roadmap for change and developing the leadership styles required to become a Lean leader:

1. Activist leadership
2. Visible leadership

3. Coaching leadership
4. Mosquito leadership

I wrote my second book, *The Simplicity of Lean*, to show the reader how they can utilise Lean thinking to transform their organisation, utilising the tools, techniques and methodologies of the Simplicity Model (a Lean practice model):

1. People engagement: culture and Kaizen
2. Process improvement: projects and Kaizen events

With this third book, *Leading Lean by Living Lean*, I've detailed out what is probably the most important part of becoming a Lean leader, which is living and practising what you preach. To do this you must believe in what you're doing, understand what it means and what you need to do, and then really do it every day. In this regard I've been influenced by David Bovis[2] and in particular his Believe, Think, Feel, Act (BTFA) model, which I cover in Chapter 1 and which has helped the engineer in me, comfortable with the Plan, Do, Check, Act (PDCA) model of Deming / Shewhart, to understand why logic and facts are very often not the principal players in the game of change.

In *Leading Lean by Living Lean* I have described how the reader may take both the PDCA and BTFA models into account and to do so I have sectioned the book into the Head, Hands and Heart:

1. Head: How you learn and understand the Lean principles and their application
2. Hands: How you practise Lean leadership on a daily basis
3. Heart: How you internalise and believe in Lean leadership

With all three books the Lean practitioner, whether aspiring or experienced, will have everything that they need to 'Lead it', 'Do it', and 'Live it'.

However, it's useful to explain why I've named them 'why to' books, when it would be more natural to call them 'how to' books. This is to recognise that I cannot tell you how to lead, do or live Lean; I can only tell you why I think that it is so important and share my knowledge, experiences, failures and successes. This book isn't so much a self-help book as a self-reflection book and the book won't change you; only you can change you!

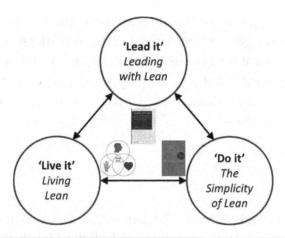

Figure 0.1 The three 'why to' Lean books

While discussing the first draft of this book with a number of trusted friends and colleagues, and in particular Jon Tudor, the author of the foreword, I was challenged to describe who the target reader of my book is. My immediate and genuine response was 'everyone, of course!', as I truly believe in the benefit that anyone can gain through the application of Lean leadership and by *Living Lean*. However, they reminded me that not everyone will be interested in a book like this, for various reasons, and that not everyone will believe in this concept.

As I pondered this predicament, it became a sort of 'circular argument'. With this book I want those who think of Lean as a toolkit, who believe that Lean can be project managed, or who argue about Lean versus Six Sigma and misunderstand the fundamental depth of impact that true Lean leadership has on an organisation, to be disabused of the notion. However, if my previous two books have not already inspired the change, then it is unlikely that person will purchase a copy of *Leading Lean by Living Lean*.

I've therefore aimed this book at those people who are 'all in'; who want to make Lean work in their organisation and are practising it at the principle level of deployment. These practitioners of Lean have come to the realisation that they need to go that extra mile to make it work and are role modelling Lean leadership in their daily lives. They are committed and want to be the best at what they do, to get results and to make a difference for themselves, their colleagues, their organisation and society. They are also the influencers, the people whose success and subsequent recommendations will drive others to read this book and to join the movement of Lean leaders.

I'm proud of the significant business success that I've helped to foster over many years through the application of Lean leadership, and in particular the significant and positive impact that it's had on the many thousands of people involved, and I really hope that you grasp the opportunity for yourself, enhancing who you are by changing what you do and the way that you do it.

Notes

1 *The Machine That Changed the World*, James P. Womack, Daniel T. Jones, Daniel Roos. Publisher: Simon & Schuster UK, ISBN-13: 978-1847370556 (www.simonandschuster.co.uk/books/The-Machine-That-Changed-the-World/James-P-Womack/9781847370556)
2 David Bovis, founder of Duxinaroe (www.duxinaroe.com/) and creator of 'The Psychology of Change'.

Acknowledgements

In my previous books I've acknowledged many of the people who've helped me to learn, develop and thrive in my career. You know who you are and I'm grateful to you.

I'll therefore limit this book's named recognition to the person who's helped me to learn, develop and thrive in both my personal and professional life, Laura, my wife.

Thank you, Laura, for your partnership and love.

About the author

Philip Holt is currently Senior Vice President, Operational Excellence at GKN Aerospace, the world's leading multi-technology tier 1 Aerospace supplier. He was formerly Vice President, Continuous Improvement at Travelport, a leading travel commerce platform, and prior to that held a number of senior Lean leadership roles with Royal Philips, most notably Head of Continuous Improvement for Philips, Head of Continuous Improvement for the Consumer Lifestyle sector, and Head of Operational Excellence, Accounting Operations. Philip was the lead author of the Philips Lean Excellence Model.

Philip has over 30 years of business experience in leadership roles spanning the customer value chain, in industry-leading companies such as GKN Aerospace, Philips, Gillette, and Travelport. During this time he has built up an impressive reputation in Lean leadership practices and is a regular speaker at industry conferences.

He studied at Manchester Metropolitan University, Warwick Business School, and the University of Pennsylvania (Wharton School).

Leading Lean by Living Lean: Changing How You Lead, Not Who You Are is his third book, following the Axiom 2020 Business Book Awards Bronze Medal winner, *The Simplicity of Lean: Defeating Complexity, Delivering Excellence* and the success of *Leading with Lean: An Experience-based Guide to Leading a Lean Transformation*.

Figures

Chapter 1

Introduction

Living Lean

In 2008 I joined the newly formed Lean team at Royal Philips, which was tasked with deploying the 'Simply Philips Operating System', and the team started its formation phase with a two-week-long 'Kaikaku experience' to Japan. It was an eye-opening visit in which we spent the first week establishing the fundamentals of the operating system and our team values, and the second week visiting world-class Lean organisations.

It was during this visit that I had the first realisation that my then nearly 20 years of experience in industry, with more than 15 years of practising Lean, had been based upon a considerable misunderstanding of what Lean really is. As an engineer, I'd enthusiastically embraced the Lean and Six Sigma toolkit and had experienced great results in the projects that I'd run, which had been enthusiastically received by senior management, and the teams that I'd been part of had been considered to have been highly successful in solving some of our largest problems.

However, I'd always wondered why the dramatic improvements in the focus area of the project had not always translated into overall improvements in the value stream, or why the results of the improvements had diminished over time. As I saw more of how those best practice companies had embedded Lean into the very fabric of their organisation, the proverbial scales started to fall from my eyes. This would become even clearer over the next few years as I gathered more evidence of how the

DOI: 10.4324/9781003251385-1

behavioural and system elements of Lean were far more important than the tools themselves.

Consider the development of what we now call Lean, which has a long history and a journey which many companies, including Toyota, began as early as the 1910s but essentially evolved from the Japanese shortage of resources and capital after World War II and specifically the way that Toyota adopted and adapted Western-quality tools to create what became the Toyota Production System (TPS) and further evolved into the Toyota Way.

Studies by Womack, Jones and others resulted in the transfer of TPS into the Western world through the many books, articles and other publications released since the late 1980s, and as part of this the term Lean was coined by John Krafcik, who was a graduate student at MIT working for Lean Enterprise Institute founder Jim Womack on the research into *The Machine That Changed the World*.[1]

The scientific approaches of the West, developed by the likes of Taylor, Shewhart, Deming et al., were adopted by the Japanese but merged with their culture, developing into an operating system built around a philosophy of people-centric problem solving. Unfortunately, as Lean was welcomed into Western practices, it was the toolkit that was readily embraced, whilst the philosophy behind its success was mostly ignored. This isn't surprising, as the philosophical elements of Lean and its implications for leadership are subtle and much less obvious than the explicit engineer-friendly toolkit, and it took me many years to fully understand what *Living Lean* really means and the importance of the intangible behavioural aspects of a Lean operating system, as opposed to the concrete tools that can be used with a misleading sense of confidence.

While we were on the Japanese Kaikaku experience, the team coined the slogan for Simply Philips:

Simple systems; Smart behaviours

Those 'smart behaviours' are the premise of this book, how *Leading Lean by Living Lean* is about developing the right behaviours to ensure that we remove the barriers to our success, those things that cause delays, frustration and excessive working hours, and ultimately make the difference between world-class performance for our customers, and the mediocre outcomes that the leadership practices of many organisations deliver.

Leading Lean by Living Lean is a guide to taking control of both your professional and personal lives, providing you with an alternative to the status quo and a means by which you can rise above the daily grind of fire-fighting.

Head, Hands and Heart

I've split the book into three main parts, looking at how we make the transition to *Living Lean* through the adoption of new behaviours: the importance of gaining intellectual buy-in (the Head); practising with the new tools and approaches (the Hands); and finally developing emotional acceptance (the Heart).

I chose the Head, Hands and Heart analogy as I've found that it resonates with many people in explaining the difference between thinking, doing and feeling. However, as David Bovis reminded me, in all cases it is 'the Head', or rather the Brain, that is processing what is happening and it is the chemical mix in both the brain and body that affects thinking, decision making, behaviours (hands) and emotions. They are not individual levers but are an integral system and, for the purpose of explanation and understanding, we may think of these as three elements but must recognise them as inter-connected, inter-dependent parts of a single system.

As you begin *Living Lean*, you will be practising using the tools that we will discuss in the book and the premise of the book is that, even if you practise the tools *on your organisation*, the only way to become a true Lean leader is to practise them *on yourself* and the way that you manage your own ways-of-working. *Living Lean* is going to help to take you through a significant but rewarding journey, from being a Lean practitioner who 'leads it' and who tells others how to 'do it', to one who shows them how to 'live it' and supports them in making the change for themselves.

Chapters 2, 3 and 4 cover the parts related to the intellectual buy-in. Chapter 2 covers how we need to think differently and change our mind-set, Chapter 3 looks at planning for the change, the change health assessment and setting a vision of the future, and finally Chapter 4 introduces the nine Lean tools to use in *Living Lean*.

In Chapters 5, 6 and 7 I encourage you to start 'using your hands'; in Chapter 5 using the nine Lean tools, avoiding procrastination and building your competence, Chapter 6 examining the subject of learning every day and showing persistence, being prepared to fail and ensuring that you follow through to the finish, and completing the section with Chapter 7, exploring Kaizen every day and the important aspects of running to standard and of looking inwards for the development of true Kaizen.

To conclude the main part of the book, Chapters 8, 9 and 10 demonstrate the significance of the heart and the emotional acceptance of the change required to be successful, exploring feeling the change in Chapter 8, winning hearts in Chapter 9 and finally *Living Lean* in Chapter 10.

To consolidate the learning, in Chapter 11 I discuss how I wrote the book using the concepts of *Living Lean* and I demonstrate how I was able to be more successful using Lean thinking, and I also talk about what I didn't include in the book and provide you with an example of my personal Hoshin.

Finally, in the epilogue in Chapter 12 I've included a LinkedIn article that I wrote in 2017 as a provocative example of how *Living Lean* requires that we are able to confront the reality of our own culpability in the problems that we have in managing our time and effectiveness. I called the article: 'If You're Too Busy, You're Not Doing It Right', and it is intended to place a mirror up for us all to reflect on how we find ourselves overloaded in our work and personal lives.

The approach of Head, Hands and Heart is well described by David Bovis in his BTFA[2] (Believe, Think, Feel, Act) model, which describes the interaction between the logical PDCA (Plan, Do, Check, Act) and emotional parts of our brain as we experience change activity.

Many readers will already be familiar with the Deming / Shewhart, or PDCA, cycle,[3] which explains how change is a cycle of:

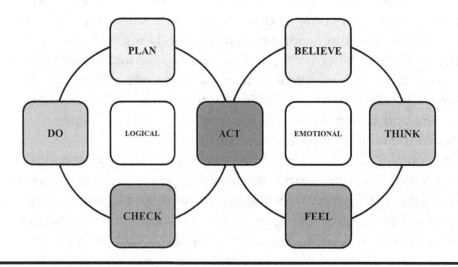

Figure 1.1 The Bovis, or BTFA, Cycle – David Bovis

1. Plan: Plan the change activity, understanding what the underlying issues are that need to be addressed and determining how to best address them.
2. Do: The implementation of the change, whereby the effort is made to execute the plan as effectively as possible.
3. Check: During and after the change has been implemented, the efficacy will be assessed to understand if the anticipated result was achieved.
4. Act: Based upon the check, either adaptations will be made and / or standards put in place to establish the new practice.

Whilst this is very logical, and especially attractive to those of us who are engineers, scientists, accountants, or other professionals who tend to deal in 1+1=2 types of problem solving, what it doesn't adequately demonstrate is how the humans in the change process react in reality, which ironically includes those of us who pride ourselves in the application of logic.

What the Bovis cycle helps to explain is that, as we run through the logical PDCA cycle, there is an emotional BTFA cycle also at play:

1. Believe: As we go through the problem solving and planning of the change, there must be a belief created that it is the right thing to do. We sometimes refer to this as stakeholder management, forming a guiding coalition, or other approaches which accept that change requires the acceptance of the people involved.
2. Think: Whilst the plan is being implemented, it is experienced and processed by the people involved. What do they think about the process of change? How does it affect them?
3. Feel: As the people experience the outcome of the change, what it means to them and how it impacts their world will evoke an emotional reaction; they will feel the impact of the change.
4. Act: Logic should drive the actions taken as an outcome of the success or failure of the change. However, in reality it is often driven emotionally and often will be contrary to what logic might suggest.

It explains why new ways-of-working, new theories or practices, which are strongly rooted in logic and fact, can take years, if not decades, to be fully accepted and adopted. It's also worth mentioning at this stage that the BTFA cycle isn't a sequential, or one-way, cycle. The brain, triggered by fear or other stimuli, can run either in the BTFA or AFTB direction.

Consider ideas such as the Earth being spherical (rather than flat), heliocentrism rather than geocentrism (the world revolving around the sun rather than the other way around), universal suffrage (the democratic vote for all), or the equality of all people under the law. All of these concepts have sound evidence and logic behind them, which was well known over many decades of unacceptance, denial and outright opposition by many in the establishments of the aristocracy, government, industry, media and religion. In fact, a great number of lives have been lost over the centuries because what was logically right was not emotionally accepted due to vested interest or, simply, complete denial.

A great example of this is that of Joseph Lister,[4] a Scottish-British surgeon who applied Louis Pasteur's advances in microbiology to champion the use of antiseptic in surgery, subsequently distinguishing him as the "father of modern surgery". Nevertheless, it wasn't something that was earned overnight, as despite overwhelming evidence of the success of his antiseptic methods, demonstrating significantly higher survival rates (lower mortality rates) for surgery patients, it took over a decade[5] for the doctors and nurses of King's College Hospital, where he was professor of surgery, to accept his work.

I'm certain that you will have your own experiences of this kind of inertia, where changes that seem clearly to be the right thing to do are either not implemented, inexplicably modified, or take an inordinate amount of time to adopt, and I hope that as you read *Leading Lean by Living Lean* you will see how you can transition to some new behaviours that will not only help you to live your life better but also help others to do so too.

PDCA – BTFA employee engagement

One of my key objectives with this book is to help you, the reader, make the changes that you want to make to meet your own improvement goals. An important element in my view is your own employee engagement, which might sound like a strange thing to say, as surely it's your organisation and your manager's job to engage you, and your job to engage the people who work for you, isn't it?

I find that an *un-Lean* way of thinking, as, whilst the organisation surely suffers from disengaged employees, the employees themselves, in this case you, suffer more. Think about it: half of your adult waking life is spent at work and so if you're disengaged from it, then it means that you are disengaged from half of your waking life! Surely if you can become more engaged with your organisation, you can become more engaged with your life?

The concept of BTFA is important to this thinking, because it can help us in determining what it is that we need from our work in order to feel good about it and hence to become more engaged with our work, colleagues, customers and organisation. For example, we can consider that there are a number of PDCA elements that, quite understandably, impact our engagement: *salary, employment conditions, work environment, travel requirements, pension, healthcare, commute, etc.* However, there are many, sometimes more important, but less tangible, BTFA elements: *your relationships with your manager and colleagues, the mission and purpose of the organisation, your perception of how you are contributing to society, how you feel when you tell people what you do and why you do it.* I'm sure that there are other things that you can think of but hopefully this helps to illustrate the importance of considering not only the tangible and logical but also the elements of your work that in many cases impact you more than those items written in your contract.

As we progress through the book, you'll read more examples of how the cognisance of the emotional elements are impacting what we do, think and feel on a daily basis and the importance of understanding and harnessing this knowledge. It's happening whether you choose to acknowledge it or not, and so it's much better to work with the model to your benefit, than to be a pawn of this invisible hand.

Hansei

Readers of my earlier books, *Leading with Lean: An Experience-based Guide to Leading a Lean Transformation*[6] and *The Simplicity of Lean: Defeating Complexity, Delivering Excellence*,[7] will be very familiar with the practice of Hansei and my strong belief in its benefits. However, I hope that those of you who have read it previously will indulge me as I share it with new readers.

From an early age, Japanese children learn what the Japanese call 'Hansei', a form of self-reflection to understand what went wrong in a given situation and to learn from it. From their first social interactions at kindergarten, when a Japanese child behaves in a way deemed unacceptable to their teacher, they will be asked to take some Hansei time to think about what they have done wrong, then explain their reflections to their teacher and what they might do differently in the future. Whilst it could be argued that children are often asked to 'think about what you've done' in Western society, it is much more common for the child to be told what it is that they did wrong and how they should adjust their behaviour to conform in the future. This differs from the approach taken with the Japanese school child.

The habit of Hansei is probably one of the key differences between the Japanese and Western way of thinking. This may go some way toward explaining why problem solving in the form of the Deming or PDCA cycle was adopted with such sustainability by a large number of Japanese companies, as you might be able to see how this supports a person through the BTFA cycle described earlier.

In the Eastern philosophical context, PDCA provided a simple method to increase the degree to which people could be respected and own their own problem solving, a way by which they could solve the problems that were causing them problems in their work. In contrast, in the West, PDCA, without the philosophical backdrop, provided logical steps to follow that became an engineering approach and another opportunity to unintentionally remove ownership from the people doing the job. Consider how 5S in the West is only 4S in the East; sustainability isn't in question, with unambiguous ownership by the team members.

Living Lean relies heavily on Hansei as a habit, as it provides a certain freedom of action, providing one with the autonomy to experiment with new approaches and to accept challenges without the fear of failure. When you reach this level of understanding and internalisation, it is a liberating experience. However, it takes some practice and persistence, especially when the work days are long and there's always more to do. To stop and take the time for Hansei when you have an overflowing email inbox and multiple meeting invitations is hard to do, although ironically it is simultaneously the time at which you need it the most.

To start you on the road to daily Hansei, and to support your development of this practice, at the end of every chapter there is a page for your reflections. Hansei is an opportunity for 'reflecting back on one's self, one's own action' and therefore provides you, the reader, with a few moments to think about how what you have just read links to your own way of working and actions.

Therefore, I would encourage that, at the end of each chapter and before reading further, you take a pen and consider what, in relation to your own way of working and actions, are:

1. Your key learning points?
2. The changes that you could make?
3. Current problems that they would help to solve?

By doing this at the end of every chapter, you will hopefully already begin *Living Lean* by becoming a continuous learner.

> *In a very real sense we have two minds, one that thinks and one that feels ~ Daniel Goleman*

Hansei

Before moving on to the next chapter, please take a few moments to reflect and consider what, in relation to your own way of working and actions, are:

Your key learning points?

The changes that you could make?

Current problems that they would help to solve?

Notes

1 *The Machine That Changed the World*, James P. Womack, Daniel T. Jones, Daniel Roos. Publisher: Simon & Schuster UK, ISBN-13: 978-1847370556 (www.simonandschuster.co.uk/books/The-Machine-That-Changed-the-World/James-P-Womack/9781847370556)
2 David Bovis, founder of Duxinaroe (www.duxinaroe.com/) and creator of 'The Psychology of Change'
3 In 1924, Walter Shewhart developed the approach to problem solving and continuous improvement that became more commonly known as either the Deming or PDCA cycle. It is a methodology which takes the user through the process of planning the change (Plan), implementing the change (Do), confirming the efficacy of the change (Check or Study) and making adaptations or changes if the results aren't as planned (Act). Deming learnt this approach from Shewhart and, despite calling it the Shewhart cycle, its popularity through Deming's teaching has resulted in most people knowing it as the Deming cycle. Source: US National Library of Medicine (www.ncbi.nlm.nih.gov/pmc/articles/PMC2464836/)
4 Joseph Lister was a British surgeon and a pioneer of antiseptic surgery. Lister promoted the idea of sterile surgery while working at the Glasgow Royal Infirmary. Lister successfully introduced carbolic acid (now known as phenol) to sterilise surgical instruments and to clean wounds. (https://en.wikipedia.org/wiki/Joseph_Lister)
5 *Hektoen International: A Journal of Medical Humanities*: Joseph Lister and the story of antiseptic surgery. (https://hekint.org/2017/01/22/joseph-lister-and-the-story-of-antiseptic-surgery/)
6 *Leading with Lean: An Experienced-based Guide to Leading a Lean Transformation.* Publisher: Vakmedianet, ISBN-13: 978-9462761445
7 *The Simplicity of Lean: Defeating Complexity, Delivering Excellence.* Publisher: Global Publisher Services; 01 edition (3rd June 2019), ISBN-13: 978-9462763227.

HEAD

1

Chapter 2

Intellectual buy-in

Thinking differently

I opened *Leading with Lean* with the metaphor of the 'Lone Violinist', using the story of the world-famous violinist Joshua Bell[1] as an example of how even the most expert professional can be ignored if they haven't created the context within which they can be heard. The key point to this is that it isn't enough to know what needs to be done to make the required change in your organisation, but rather, people must be brought along and be willing to 'pay to listen to you'.

People are most likely to favour people who conform to the perceived consensus and are more likely to hire people who they identify as being similar to them. These biases mean that in many cases organisations put leaders of change in place who are very much invested in, and part of, the status quo. This risks that the very people charged with transforming the organisation for the world of tomorrow are:

Same agents, not change agents

Similarly, the majority of people labour under the disadvantage of what is called 'conformity bias'[2], a bias referring to our tendency to take cues for proper behaviour in most contexts from the actions of others rather than exercising our own independent judgement. This creates a contradiction for the person leading change in the organisation, as they must simultaneously

DOI: 10.4324/9781003251385-3

be someone who thinks differently and is willing to challenge the status quo but, at the same time, able to engage people in listening to their vision of the future, breaking through the cognitive biases and establishing the prospect of the new normal.

Thinking differently is a riskier strategy than thinking the same as those around you, but then no-one ever made a breakthrough by playing it safe. *Living Lean* might not be as risky as base jumping, but it isn't for those who want to 'fit in' their organisation's current norms; it's for those who want to create the organisation's new norms.

Changing mind-set

Before the sentiment of the book becomes too much around changing others' thinking, let's remember that *Living Lean* is about how you, the reader, can make your own change. The outcome of this will be that your ability to influence others and lead the change in your organisation will significantly increase but, just like the emergency instructions on an aeroplane, please put on your own oxygen mask before helping others, metaphorically speaking.

To assist you with this, I've created a five-point change self-assessment that you can use to test where you are in terms of your need to change your thinking and approach. The idea of this is that you complete it for yourself now and, at the end of the book, update it to see where you have made changes in your thinking. You can then use it on an ongoing basis and, once your oxygen mask is firmly on, you could potentially use it with your colleagues. Combined with the practice of Hansei, I'm certain that it will support you on your way to *Living Lean*.

The statements are deliberately written in a manner to evoke an emotional response, which is why the scale is based upon agreement and not frequency or another more scientific measure. What I want you to do is feel the statements and mark what your level of agreement is with them. I'd like you to provide three ratings:

1. Draw a triangle for where you feel that you are now (at the point of reading this chapter).
2. When you've completed the book draw a circle to see how you've changed in the time that it took you to complete the next 10 chapters.

3. Finally, decide where you want to get to as a target state and draw a square.

Whilst the target state might be implied as being a 'Strongly Agree' for all of the statements, I want you to decide how you feel about it after you've finished the book. I'm not going to tell you what you need to do to attain your target state, and it'll be interesting for you to reflect on whether your Head and Heart agree!

The reader might ask why these five statements are the most important ones and why there aren't other elements on the change self-assessment. The simple answer is that I wrote down over 20 statements in total when devising this and quite clearly these five were by far the most pertinent and important in my change journey.

By now it will be clear that Hansei has been a significant part of my personal and professional development and therefore ranks easily as my number one change success factor. Coming a very close second is the management of time, as its waste is the largest opponent of success that one can find and so the willingness to tackle effectiveness with structure must feature highly in this list. Thirdly, the understanding and acceptance of the impact of human emotion is central to *Living Lean*, as is managing the emotion of 'quick fixes' and 'firefighting' when problem solving. Last, but by no means least, is the acceptance of the need for personal change that

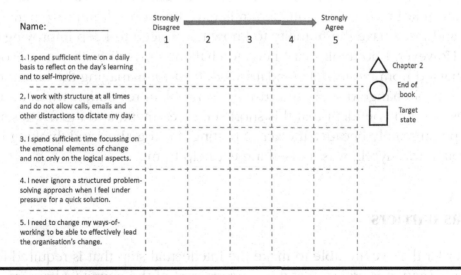

Figure 2.1 5-point change self-assessment

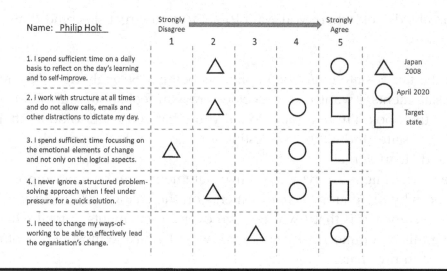

Figure 2.2   The author's 5-point change self-assessment

is required in order to embrace the internalisation of Lean leadership that is required for success.

In case you're wondering where I would rate myself on this self-assessment, I've undertaken a retrospective view of myself from 2008 to today (April 2020), which shows that, despite being someone who prided himself in self-reflection, structure, problem solving and a focus on continually improving, the trip to Japan, and the launch of Simply Philips, demonstrated to me that I was far from where I needed to be.

Currently I believe that my Hansei time, practised for over 10 years, means that I now spend sufficient reflective time on self-improvement (test 1), and that I have the humility to know that I need to keep improving (test 5). However, I do think that I need to challenge myself further on becoming distracted from my leader standard work (test 2), managing the emotional aspects of change (test 3) and rushing to problem resolution when under pressure. I'm confident that this short self-assessment, and the five tests, will help you mainly because the act of putting this together, and thinking it through for myself, was in itself a great help to me.

Bias barriers

In order that we are able to make the intellectual step that is required for *Living Lean*, it is critical that we are cognisant of the cognitive barriers

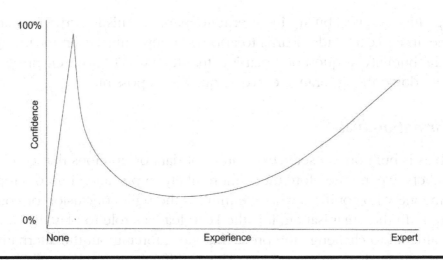

Figure 2.3 The Dunning–Kruger effect

that we have developed over the many years of our existence. It's not that we can immediately recognise them and rid ourselves of them, as they are deeply rooted and in many cases reside in our blind spot, but by acknowledging their existence, understanding some of what they do and why we have them, we can at least be on the watch out for them and try to avoid their pitfalls.

To explain what they are, bias barriers are those inherent human psychological traits that get in the way of us changing our thinking. Christopher Dwyer Ph.D wrote in the Psychology Today blog[3] about the common biases that we must first be cognisant of if we're to attempt to free ourselves of them. I would recommend reading the blog, as it has 12 in total, but here are some of the key ones that I have found to be a challenge to *Living Lean*:

The Dunning–Kruger effect

This phenomenon might best be described in layman's terms as when somebody 'doesn't know what they don't know' or perhaps even 'a little knowledge is dangerous'. It is where somebody has learned a little about a subject and sees it as much simpler than it really is but, and this is the crucial element, is unaware of the additional complexity and therefore speaks to the subject with an air of authority.

I'm sure that you must have seen this in your activities, whereupon a colleague learns a little about a subject and suddenly becomes an 'expert', regurgitating the vocabulary in an erudite manner. This is a true barrier to change and a Lean leader learns to approach new subjects and learning with the humility to question what it is that they don't know, ensuring that they get down the ignorance curve as quickly as possible.

Confirmation bias

This bias is built on the seductive nature of data or opinions that confirm our beliefs. We are therefore much more likely to pay attention to a report or someone who confirms what we think is the right conclusion or course of action. In the organisation, it is the Lean leader's role to play the devil's advocate and to challenge the prevailing view, forcing out the alternative data or perspectives on the subject. This is difficult, as it relates to Chapter 1 and the challenge of being the person to question the group's thinking.

Nevertheless, as hard as it might be to confront others, it is even more of a test when it comes to challenging oneself, as you will find yourself to be a stubborn opponent. You have innate, long-term views that are entrenched in your very being, and to tell yourself that you might be wrong is not something that any of us find easy to do.

As Dr. Dwyer states in his blog:

> *Remember, we are cognitively lazy – we don't like changing our knowledge (schema) structures and how we think about things.*

A further insight into this comes from David Bovis, who explained to me how changing our mind about ourselves is energy intensive (has to feed the neurogenesis process) and our brain is structured to conserve energy, which makes challenging oneself one of the hardest things to do, but on the other hand one of the most liberating and beneficial things when we learn how to do it and make it a habit. In colloquial terms, anything worth doing takes effort!

Self-serving bias

This bias is one where we see our successes as due to our hard work, whilst our failures are the work of others. In the workplace we feel that things that we can't get done well are due to our boss', or colleagues', actions, whereas the project that hits all of its targets was completely due to our endeavours. Colloquially one might say that we are the father to our successes, whilst failures are the bastard child of others.

This is also one of the biases that most often gets in the way of Kaizen, as team members will initially come up with 'Kaizen' that others should do to fix their problems. Only when we can get past the self-serving bias can we encourage our colleagues to look at their own problems and implement true Kaizen.

Living Lean means being the father to both our successes and our failures, accepting the outcomes and problem solving to understand what went well, what didn't go well, and what the root causes were.

The sunk cost fallacy

If you have invested hours of work and lots of money into an activity, it is more likely that you will continue to work on it than if you had spent little time and little money on it. This is due to the bias that we take into account past actions in making future decisions, whereas only the future investments required for the outcome should be taken into account. This is one of the reasons why people continue to invest in projects and other ventures, even when the likelihood of success is logically low. This is another great example of how emotions impact decisions just as much, if not more than, the logic of the situation.

An example related to this is the Monte Carlo fallacy, which is based upon the probability of winning on a roulette wheel when betting on red or black. If the last four spins of the roulette wheel had come up black, the majority of people would predict that the odds of the next spin coming up red were more likely than for black. However, the odds remain at 50:50 regardless of how many times it has come up black previously. This is called the Monte Carlo fallacy after the 1913 event in the Monte Carlo Casino whereupon the ball fell on black 26 times in a row, with gamblers losing millions in the misguided belief that it must land red next!

In my personal experiences I have often had to stop investments in technology, both IT and machinery, which has caused discord amongst those people heavily invested in the sunk cost of the projects. In many cases it's not that they're not good ideas per se, but that we need and can get a lot more benefit in the short term by putting in place the 'brilliant basics' of Lean thinking before we invest in the technology.

The decline bias

In this bias, people see the future as less rosy than the past, as they want the world around them to fit their current view of it, and this bias is a great barrier to change. The world is easier to process and to be engaged with when it makes sense to us, and so we don't really want to think differently about how our world should run. *Living Lean* means being prepared to change ourselves, and not just ask others to move to our world view.

This is frequently found in a lot of Western businesses that were historically successful in a previous era of pseudo-monopoly or low competition, or where technological advances in recent years have disrupted them. There will be many team members who remember the 'good old days' and, whilst much of it will be nostalgia, there will still be good reason for their feelings. The key to tackling this is to tap into it as a case for change; if we want the good times back we need to find a new way, and we want them to be part of its creation.

In-group bias

This is where we tend to favour those in our own group over others. From a *Living Lean* perspective this is important because it can influence us into the 'it won't work here' mentality and therefore hold us back from adopting those best practices that other groups, or industries, have successfully adopted. The Lean leader will regularly look outside of their own group to understand what new and innovative ways there might be to solve chronic issues that they, their organisation, or even their industry, might suffer from.

As you've read through these, I hope that you've recognised your own culpability in allowing them to influence your thinking. If not, please re-read and maybe do further study, as I promise you that you suffer from them, as we all do, and it is not a good or bad thing, but a human condition. As with all things in Lean leadership, acceptance and making problems visible is not about blame or identifying failure but about accepting the problems and solving them, whether it be a quality issue on a part or a mind-set that gets in the way of our own success.

Bias barriers are an intellectual impediment of success that cannot be eradicated but the effects of which can be managed with vigilance, ensuring that we minimise their impact.

You don't pay to watch logic

Throughout the book I'll espouse the importance of the BTFA model, the emotional considerations that we must make to be successful in any change that we make, and how important it is to first make that change for ourselves. However, at this early stage I wonder whether you yet believe me, or if you're thinking that intellect is all that is required to make a change happen? Have I touched your emotions around this or are you still reading this with the sceptical logic that I might expect you to? In case the latter is true let me try, as I often do, to use an analogy to emphasise my point.

Think about sport, something that the vast majority of us can connect with. Whatever your sport of choice might be, to play or spectate, could you argue that your connection and enthusiasm for that sport is truly and wholly logical? I don't think so, in fact I would guess that it is far more emotional than logical, especially if the sports team that you support is less than successful.

That is the case for me, being a life-long Bolton Wanderers supporter, a team that, if logic applied, would not be the choice of many. Bolton were a founder member of the English Football League (one of 12) and have a long history of ups and downs and, when I started supporting them in the early 1980s, had just begun a decade-long drop from the top division to the bottom one (the fourth level). Nevertheless, despite that fact there was never an alternative choice for me, despite living close to Manchester (City and United), Liverpool (Liverpool FC and Everton), Leeds, and a number of other more successful teams within easy reach. I was born in Bolton and therefore they would be my team and Burnden Park, their stadium, my place of pilgrimage every other Saturday afternoon (and sometimes mid-week). I've watched them play in every division in the English professional leagues, back up to the top (Premiership) for a decade or so, and then back down to the bottom division again (as of December 2021, they're currently in tier 3 of 4).

I'm sure that you could make a logical case for being a Bolton fan, as it's certainly not boring and we've had some fantastic players and managers (coaches) over the past four decades, but it truly is an emotional attachment that I have to them, one that I'm sure many readers can relate to with their team of choice, in whichever sport it might be. It's similar if you think about how a nation becomes enthralled in major sporting events, such as the Olympics, whereby previously unknown sportsmen and women become overnight celebrities due to a national outpouring of positive emotion towards what they've achieved for 'our' country.

Consider the stars and celebrities that we adore and who earn millions of dollars per year for playing sports, starring in movies, performing as artists, or hosting a TV talk show. Why do we place these people on a pedestal above scientists or engineers? Surely it's not because of a logical assessment of their value to society? Why do we generally see the frontman or woman of a band as the superstar? Does their singing prowess logically put them above the thousands of hours of practice and technical ability of the guitarist or drummer?

I think that in all of these examples you should be able to see that it's the emotional attachments that we make that drive our behaviour and our decision-making processes and, even when you think about something that ought to be much more logical, such as the stock market, it's clear that the language used, about market sentiment, investor activism and the like, demonstrates the significant emotion that plays into the investment decisions that people make every day, and we see this in the pseudo-celebrity of CEOs such as Elon Musk et al.

If you reflect on this during your Hansei time, I'd like you to think about where your and your colleague's decisions are being influenced by the BTFA cycle and how you can consider this more in your change leadership. Gaining that balance between PDCA and BTFA will make you a better (Lean) leader and also help you to more effectively navigate the challenges that you face and the illogical intransigence that you will often encounter, even within yourself.

Hansei

Before moving onto the next chapter, please take a few moments to reflect and consider what, in relation to your own way of working and actions, are:

Your key learning points?

The changes that you could make?

Current problems that they would help to solve?

Notes

1 Pearls Before Breakfast, *Washington Post*, 8th April 2007: (www.washingtonpost. com/lifestyle/magazine/pearls-before-breakfast-can-one-of-the-nations-great-musicians-cut-through-the-fog-of-a-dc-rush-hour-lets-find-out/2014/09/23/ 8a6d46da-4331-11e4-b47c-f5889e061e5f_story.html)
2 Conformity Bias, McCombs School of Business, Ethics Unwrapped. (https:// ethicsunwrapped.utexas.edu/video/conformity-bias)
3 12 Common Biases that Affect How We Make Everyday Decisions, Christopher Dwyer Ph.D., Psychology Today. (www.psychologytoday.com/gb/blog/thoughts-thinking/201809/12-common-biases-affect-how-we-make-everyday-decisions)

Chapter 3

Planning the change

VCRSP

Planning the change is an important part of making your transition to *Living Lean* but it is only one of the five elements required to make your change a success. The VCRSP model[1] is one which I use extensively and is a great barometer for the health of any change activity that you are leading. However, it can also be utilised for your own change, as it is just as important to ensure that you have all five in place as you go on this voyage.

Vision

Do you know what the future could look like for you? What will *Living Lean* mean for you? Using the self-assessment that you undertook in Chapter 2, reading this book and practising your Hansei should provide you with the insight that you need but you ultimately need to have pulled it together into a clear view of the future that you're aiming for. This will be a vision of the future that's allied to your newly acquired acceptance of the BTFA cycle and the human factors involved in its attainment. Creating your personal vision is as important as developing the organisational vision that you will support.

DOI: 10.4324/9781003251385-4

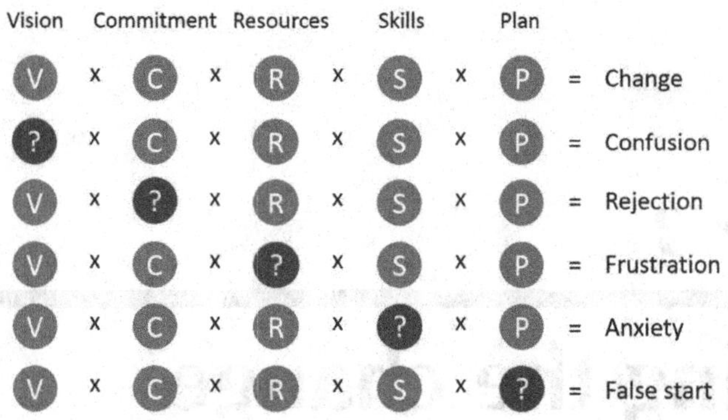

Vision		Commitment		Resources		Skills		Plan		
V	x	C	x	R	x	S	x	P	=	Change
?	x	C	x	R	x	S	x	P	=	Confusion
V	x	?	x	R	x	S	x	P	=	Rejection
V	x	C	x	?	x	S	x	P	=	Frustration
V	x	C	x	R	x	?	x	P	=	Anxiety
V	x	C	x	R	x	S	x	?	=	False start

Figure 3.1   The VCRSP model

Commitment

Are you truly committed to this change? Is it really something that you are willing to put the effort into and avoid distraction? How will you avoid a loss of motivation in the future? Are you willing to learn more about the human factors and psychology of change that will make it a success?

One of the biggest psychological barriers to making a change as significant as *Living Lean* is seeing the new approach to your work (and life) as additional work, more effort. This 'on top of' mentality, the idea that Lean thinking is something to be applied when you have the time to do it, is a phenomenon that prevails at all levels of an organisation. I'll cover this in more detail later in the book, but for now, suffice to say that it's really important to consider whether your commitment to the change extends to both the good times and the hard times. In short, is it going to be a hobby or a vocation?

This, and the other questions, must all be positively answered and constantly tested as you progress.

Resources

The main resource for this transformation is you, but you will need to ensure that you are willing to invest the time into it that is required; for reading this book (and other ones), for Hansei, for trying out the new tools and methodologies, for problem solving and for learning the new skills that you will require.

However, as you progress on your *Living Lean* journey you will aim to bring others along, colleagues who are willing to adopt and support you in this. Remember, whilst this book is focussed on your own adoption of Lean thinking, it is also about your leadership development, and a big part of that is taking others along with you, helping them to improve their own ways-of-working. Understanding whether you're doing this is important as you progress.

Skills

In order to make the change, you will need to learn some new skills, and you have a number of resources available to you. Hopefully this book, *Leading with Lean*, *The Simplicity of Lean*, and the many other great publications out there will support you in this but, ultimately, it is through your own efforts and practice that these skills will be learned. The 10,000 hours rule for a new skill[2] has been hotly disputed but it is clear that the only way to get good at something is to put in the practice and to learn from the successes and failures that it will bring. However, the important element for me is that it isn't an 'all or nothing' effort – as you learn the new skills you will start to gain benefit, and as you use them more and become better at them, you will gain even more benefit. Learning skills, if they are the right ones for the change that you want to make, will become less about the effort of learning, and much more about the benefits of their practice.

Plan

Once we have all of the first four elements in place we must, of course, have a plan. For your personal transformation this doesn't need to be a complex Microsoft project plan but should be something that is clear and visual and can be tracked for progress. I personally use an online tracker, Kanbanflow[3], which allows me to take my plan with me as I travel with my work. However, if you are in a fixed office or work from home regularly, the use of a tracker on the wall, paper-based with 'post-it notes', is a fantastic way to manage the plan.

As part of the plan, don't forget to include a way of tracking your progress, and I don't mean in terms of action items completed but, rather, your journey in the change from a PDCA to a BTFA perspective, the emotional aspect. I realise the irony of using a PDCA-style plan to track the change to BTFA thinking, but the important point here is that it's not a choice between the two but, rather, an understanding of their interaction and considerations is required.

Unfortunately, of the five elements it is the skills part that has received the most focus over the years. It feels much more tangible, can be put into nicely packaged training courses, sold by consultancy firms, rewarded with certificates or belts, and measured as a key performance indicator. This might go some small way to explaining why we have an abundance of Lean / Continuous Improvement / Six Sigma certified people but not a wealth of operational excellence.

A vision of the future

What should your vision of the future look like? What is it going to mean for you? The answers to these questions will ultimately be personal but my advice would be that there should be a central framework, a skeleton if you will, on which you place the body of your vision.

The vision framework will help you to set your vision in terms of the three components of *Living Lean*: personal effectiveness, problem solving and continuous improvement. In the next chapter I will cover the tools to use in each of these components but let's first discuss the overall outcome that you might want to aim for from each:

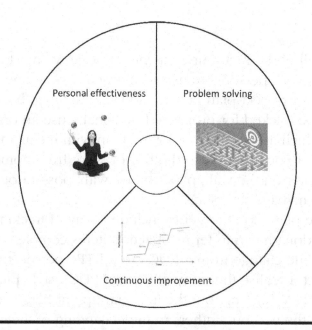

Figure 3.2   The vision framework

Personal effectiveness

Being effective on a daily basis should not be confused with being efficient. This isn't about becoming robotic in your way of working. Quite the contrary, it's about freeing up the time to do everything that you want to do, so that you can spend less time processing emails, sitting in meetings and working on the wrong things, and more time speaking with colleagues, team members, customers, suppliers, etc., making decisions and solving the problems that will grow the business and deliver success. There's more to come on this but, if you've not yet come to the realisation that Lean is about creativity and not the mundane, then I hope that you've reached this point of understanding by the end of the book and that you have a vision of personal effectiveness that will help to free you up to achieve the goals that you want to.

Problem solving

Our daily lives are about problem solving, whether it be navigating the morning commute in the most effective way, solving a major quality issue that is preventing production release, growing sales with a customer, or developing a new product. Whatever the problem might be, it is important that we solve those problems in the most effective way, both reducing the resolution time and increasing the efficacy of the solution. Unfortunately, the natural human reaction to pressurised situations is to rush to solutions, rather than understanding the problem, undertaking root cause analysis, and putting in place countermeasures to those root causes. With a solid approach to problem solving, you will make a big step towards *Living Lean*.

Continuous improvement

There is a common misconception regarding continuous improvement, which is that it is only about incremental improvement. In fact, continuous improvement is about improvement that is ongoing and never-ending, without backsliding or loss of focus.

There are two diagrams that I use to illustrate two important concepts of continuous improvement:

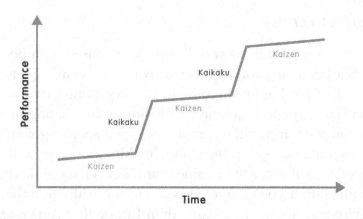

Figure 3.3   Continuous improvement illustrated

1. Continuous improvement illustrated shows that it's not only about the small improvements but also large improvements, what in Lean terms are called Kaizen and Kaikaku, respectively.
2. Continuous improvement versus discontinuous improvement demonstrates that improvement is only continuous when it is locked in with standards and built upon, something that many find hard to do and is why most, if not all, organisations do improvement activity but only a few actually do continuous improvement. However, this 'locking in' of standards must run in parallel with the re-wiring of the brain, as if the change is rejected psychologically, no amount of 'logical' standards will act as an antidote.

Living Lean means that every day we will make improvements to our methods, improving our effectiveness through rigorous problem solving, resulting in new standardised ways-of-working.

You might have realised the dichotomy that I faced at this point, as I'm using tools, the logical approach, to provide you with a methodology to change behaviours based upon emotions and deep-rooted beliefs. What I'm striving to do as I go through this process is to measure my use of language to engender the understanding of the need to feel the change as you utilise these approaches. Please take some time to reflect upon that, and really feel how you are responding to the concepts and principles that I'm explaining.

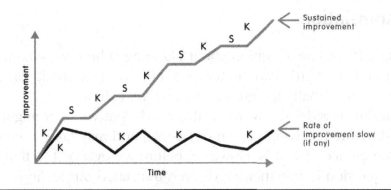

Figure 3.4   Continuous improvement versus discontinuous improvement

I love it when a plan comes together

Whilst it's important to plan your change, it doesn't need to be a military exercise and should be done in a way that works for you. It's also important to recognise that this will be an iterative process, as your brain starts to grow neurons and create a new lens by which 'good' is viewed.

Whether you decided to use Microsoft Project, an online tool, a notebook, a whiteboard planner, it doesn't really matter, use whichever tool works best for you. The really important thing is that you assure the balance of all five of the VCRSP elements in place. Planning the change means that you've established what your vision for change is, what *Living Lean* will be for you; you've made the commitment to see the transition through, putting your time and effort into it, practising the skills that you need to develop, and iteratively developing a plan, following it through to completion. Whilst doing so you'll feel the effects of it, and it will be essential to try to understand what this means in terms of the challenges that you are experiencing to your deeply held ideals.

This is a commitment to fundamentally improving how you work and your daily personal behaviours, and should not be underestimated. Like any plan it will not survive the 'first shot of battle' fully intact, and so you will iterate the plan as you cycle through PDCA and BTFA, and practise your new skills. The important thing is that you persevere and demonstrate that the C in VCRSP is truly in place.

Lost in translation

An important BTFA consideration about planning is how we communicate our ideas to others, particularly in terms of how we feel about something, which can create a challenge greater than we may think.

We typically consider the way that the words that we utter might be understood by the receiving person or people, and may take some time to consider our choice of words. However, before we even get to that point, there's the question of whether we've even translated our feelings into the correct words for ourselves. What do I mean by that, you might ask? They're our feelings and so surely we know best how to describe them?

The problem that we encounter is that the part of our brain that processes our feelings (the limbic system) is non-verbal; it cannot create the words that we need to describe the feelings. Instead, the logical part of your brain (the cerebrum) must translate those feelings into what you consider to be the right vocabulary to describe them. This is tricky and you will not necessarily be that practised in describing your feelings, especially if your profession is one of 'logic and reason' (although by now you've probably come to realise the idea of logic and reason professions to be somewhat of a myth), or if you feel inhibited by a culture which frowns upon emotional descriptors, especially those perceived to be negative. It's therefore likely that you will choose logical and rational words to try to describe how you feel about the subject and utilise those to communicate to the audience / receiver of your message.

The receiving person will then decide the meaning of your words as they interpret them, sometimes even more complicated by the fact that they might be a second or third speaker of the language used, and this will trigger an emotional response to their interpretation, influenced by their current emotional state, which will also have influenced the interpretation of the words. This communication route runs either cyclically or in one direction, dependent upon whether it is a conversation or a sending communication. You may infer from this that the cyclical approach is the best one, as it will allow clarifications to be made and a sharing of interpretations through feedback and questioning. This is true in the ideal sense but may also fail miserably if there is a lack of trust or good intention between the two parties and negative meanings might be inferred even where they are unintended.

How do we tackle this translation of feelings issue? The first suggestion that I have is to work on using more emotionally descriptive language. For example, if you feel that a course of direction is not right, admit if you don't have the facts around it yet or if you've even not got a sense of it being right or wrong and explain that it is the case. Don't wrap up a feeling in language intended to imply that you have a logical reason for how you feel. Secondly, question and ask probing questions to understand someone's meaning. Ask them to expand on what they are saying even if, or rather especially if, you think that you understand them. By having dialogue which is more honest in its language we can open up our communication to be more connected with the intent of the sender in their words.

However, this isn't easy and requires you, as a leader, to lead the culture change required. As with everything in this book, it begins with you and can be something that you first experiment with in your team or even in already trusted one-to-one relationships. As you and your colleagues gain confidence in the approach, it can be discussed and trialled with other colleagues, and so on, and you can learn and adapt as necessary, using your Hansei time to reflect upon how it might be helping you to develop your relationships, strengthen trust and bolster success.

Many of the guidelines for effective communications are essentially trying to countermeasure the issues that I have raised, and you can find these quite easily with a Google search or from your organisation's communication department. However, I don't feel that we spend enough time really considering the emotional–logical–logical–emotional communication route that the meaning needs to traverse and instead talk too much of communication in terms of the logical (PDCA).

Each time we communicate, there is an invisible translation continuum whereby *Beliefs* stimulate *Feelings* that are converted into *Thoughts*. These thoughts are then translated into Language, which is subsequently interpreted by the receiver, who then reverses the sequence into *Thoughts–Feelings–Beliefs*. This interaction of PDCA–BTFA is complex and it's no wonder that we experience so many challenges with change management as a result of communication and understanding.

I'm not going to pretend that all of this is easy, or that I've fully 'cracked the code'. This book is a good example of that, as it's probably still very much in the realms of the rational and logical language and, despite my feelings and emotions towards the importance of effective Lean leadership, and of *Living Lean* being very strongly and deeply rooted in my belief system, I'm sure that I'm still biased towards describing my feelings and experiences to you in a more logical style. It is one of the reasons that I encourage you to undertake Hansei at the end of each chapter, to at least provide some time for you to properly digest my words and hopefully facilitate the emotional interpretation.

> *Failing to plan is planning to fail*
> Proverbial wisdom with an anonymous origin

Hansei

Before moving onto the next chapter, please take a few moments to reflect and consider what, in relation to your own way of working and actions, are:

Your key learning points?

The changes that you could make?

Current problems that they would help to solve?

Notes

1 The VCRSP model: VCRSP Matrix adapted from Knoster, T. (1991) Presentation in TASH Conference. Washington, D.C.
2 *Outliers: The Story of Success*, Malcolm Gladwell. Publisher: Penguin (24th June 2009), ISBN-13: 978-0141036250
3 Kanbanflow is an online tool for tracking projects or activities in a visual and easy to use Kanban board. (www.Kanbanflow.com)

Chapter 4

The tools to use

Whilst there are many tools in the Lean toolkit, I have selected three tools for each of the three components of the vision framework. This provides you with nine tools that I believe will support you well in your new approach. Nevertheless, please remember that this is not about mechanistically applying the tools in a certain order, it's about applying these tools to your own way-of-working, about the changes that you'll make to your personal working practices, not about the application of these tools more generally. You're going to put your own oxygen mask on first.

The way that you think and feel about your belief in the need to improve your day-to-day behaviours (as per the self-assessment against the five tests) will determine how and if you act to make any personal changes. This is the BTFA aspect of change and provides a good example of just why the emotion of change must be considered at every step of any transformation, in every person involved. The emotional reaction to change is very different when it is a free choice made individually, versus imposed change, and that emotional response determines the attitude and reaction provoked.

This chapter is a good example of this point, as it is quite a 'dry' chapter, covering the tools and standards. How can I be talking about changing behaviour and the emotional elements of change if I'm then going to apply the tools? Surely tools and standards are, by definition, PDCA thinking. However, this illustrates the message that I've been attempting to get across about the interactivity and iterative nature of PDCA–BTFA and the Head, Hands and Heart, which all effectively come back to the functioning of

DOI: 10.4324/9781003251385-5

the brain and your currently embedded beliefs, likes, dislikes, prejudices, preferences, and so on.

I'm a heavy user of analogies, and sports are one of my favourite subjects, and so I'm going to use one about football (soccer) to illustrate the importance of tools and standards as part of the ingredients of successfully *Living Lean*. Consider this as you read through this chapter and the subsequent elements of the tools and standards.

I played football (soccer) for many years and enjoyed it immensely. I played some Saturday, but mostly Sunday, amateur local league and was an enthusiastic participant at almost every game, come rain or shine. As is the policy of the Football Association (and FIFA), the rules that I played under were identical to those of the higher-level amateur, semi-professional and professional leagues. So this begs the question that, if my team mates, the opposition players, the referee and I had to use the same standards (the rules, including the pitch / field dimensions, size of the ball, goal size, etc.) and had access to the same tools and technologies (football boots, ball, kit, etc.), why was it that there were many hundreds of thousands, if not millions, of people who were better than me at the game? Why is it that a player like Lionel Messi, one of the world's greatest footballers, looks like he's playing a different game compared to me? Surely standards stifle innovation and creativity, making everyone the same, almost robotic-like?

Or could it be that, rather than being a barrier to creativity, standards 'lock in' the solutions to problems that we've already solved and that our attention should be on the focussed and dedicated practice that will make us as good as we possibly can be? I think so, and I would encourage you to utilise the tools and standards throughout this book that are tried and tested, and use your talent, experience, intellect and creativity, just as Messi would, to be the best that you can be at whatever you might do.

Personal effectiveness

Time management

There are a number of time management techniques that I covered in *The Simplicity of Lean*, and the other two tools in this section are also, in effect, time management tools. However, I want to start with the Pomodoro technique.

The Pomodoro technique is not new, having been developed by Francesco Cirillo in the late 1980s. It is named after the Italian word for tomato, due to the predominance of tomato-shaped kitchen timers in the 1980s. The thinking behind the technique is that a human can work best focussed for periods of 25 minutes on a single task, fully concentrated and avoiding any distractions. In brief, the process is:

■ Decide on the task to be done.
■ Set the Pomodoro timer to 25 minutes.
■ Work on the task until the timer rings.
■ Take a short break (3–5 minutes).
■ After four Pomodori, take a longer break (15–30 minutes).

I have used this technique for a few years now and it is not an exaggeration to describe it as revolutionary as it provides the necessary rest for your brain to 'decompress'. It can be very difficult to do this in times of high pressure or when you're under a tight deadline, as the natural instinct is to keep working and to not take a break.

Under these circumstances it is even more important to take a break and as you practise using this technique you will experience the additional mental energy, more effective creativity and increased work rate that the breaks provide for you. Nevertheless, for you to do this you'll need to believe in the science and that this will truly make a difference for you. That will be the difference between a narrative of: 'That sounds great, but I'm far too busy to stop every 25mins, I'd get nothing done', and one of: 'If that's the case, it's imperative I do this as much as possible; where is my stopwatch, I'm setting it for 25 mins?'

Figure 4.1 The Pomodoro technique of working time intervals

Personal Kanban

A Kanban is a card system used in Lean manufacturing to visually and simply manage the flow of information and materials through the supply chain in a way that promotes the creation of inventory only in response to customer demand, what is known as a 'pull system'. This approach has been adapted for project management and also for use by individuals, and is called a 'personal Kanban'. This approach is relatively simple to set up but the challenge, as with most Lean tools, is the discipline around its application. There are variations on the design and nuances on the 'rules' but the approach that I take is:

- The planning cycle is weekly.
- Work is categorised as: standard work (daily, weekly, monthly, quarterly) or 'to do' items.
- The ratio of standard work to ad hoc 'to do' items will depend upon your role in the organisation, but it should certainly be more standard work than ad hoc.
- Personally I maintain it at around 70% standard work but with the caveat that I see ad hoc tasks as a 'miss' in my standard work and a problem to solve.
- At the end of the week, I prioritise the items due in the coming week based upon due date and importance.
- At this time I also review the next month's due items to orientate on upcoming activities and preparation requirements.
- I plan the activities, based upon their priority, across the available time during the week and review already planned activity and meetings to establish if they are congruent with the priorities.
- Where there is insufficient time available for all of the week's priorities, I consider possible countermeasures and ultimately discuss with the 'customers' of the activities the possibilities to reschedule / reprioritise as necessary, or for delegation or support from colleagues.
- I execute the priorities using the 'personal Kanban' board, moving the activities from the 'things to do' column into the 'doing', with the doing having a maximum of three 'live' items at a time.
- The reason for the maximum of three items is the acceptance that sometimes responses from others will be required before an item can be closed and therefore you may need to move between the three items during the day.

- As a 'doing' item is completed a new item moves into the 'doing' column.
- Daily (day start is usually the best) I review progress and ensure that any required adjustments are made.

Using a personal Kanban will provide you with a much more effective way of managing your activities and keeping to your commitments. If we're honest with ourselves, we all tend to work on the things that are easier, more interesting, in which we're personally invested, sometimes to the detriment of those things that are more important. Personal Kanban ensures that we work on the right things at the right time.

Nevertheless, recognising that there are altering priorities and asking people if things can be delayed is easier for leaders than it is for followers, as a subordinate is much more likely to capitulate and agree to a change to a planned schedule than they are to say, no, you need to get this done or turn up and be fully present (hold their boss to task). This is the 'social' part of BTFA, the consideration of the environmental dimensions that have an effect on activities and the different adoption of principles in different hierarchical layers of the organisation.

The assumption made by those with the power in any power-distance relationship is "if I can do it, so can others", failing to recognise how that attitude contributes to the reasons why other people find it more difficult to emulate the behaviours of leaders, that they don't have the same power, and therefore levels of confidence to make the same choices or have the same effect on others around them.

Meeting management: Terms of Reference

A Terms of Reference (TOR) can be used for both recurring and one-off meetings and in any effective organisation should be willingly adopted. It is extremely important that you focus on meetings that deliver fact-based, customer-orientated results. Whilst your meetings will be with others, you can take the initiative to introduce these to the meetings that you run and insist upon them for the meetings that you are invited to. You'll be pleasantly surprised how enthusiastically the TOR is adopted by others once they experience the improvement that it brings to their meetings.

As I wrote in *The Simplicity of Lean*, meetings are a major drain on workers' time, and there are some scary statistics. According to *The Muse*[1]:

- $37 billion per year is wasted in unproductive meetings.
- There are 25 million meetings per day in the USA.
- 15% of an organisation's collective time is spent in meetings, a figure that has increased every year since 2008.
- Middle managers spend 35% of their time in meetings, for senior managers it's 50%.
- People spend up to four hours per week preparing for status update meetings.
- Executives consider 67% of all meetings to be a failure.

If you recognise these symptoms, it's therefore perhaps not surprising that you could put in place some relatively simple countermeasures:

1. ***Before scheduling a meeting, first consider whether it is necessary.*** This might sound like common sense, but we are often so involved in things that we call a meeting as a 'knee jerk' reaction. Taking a breath and running the problem-solving process before calling the meeting will ensure that you only call necessary meetings and only invite the right people.

2. ***Ensure that the meeting is part of a process.*** A meeting should be a moment whereby team updates are given, problem solving undertaken, or decisions made. If there's no clear purpose for the meeting as a milestone in a process it ought not to proceed. David Bovis challenged me on this point, asking about the BTFA elements of meetings, where it might be that the meeting is there to reassure people, to communicate to them, to understand concerns. It is a valid and extremely important challenge and my response to that is that it is still part of a process, the change management process, whereby we're ensuring that we are adequately managing the organisation through the emotionally charged process of change. This has been a key learning for me, that processes will always be a combination of PDCA and BTFA and in some cases might be more heavily geared towards the BTFA element.

3. ***Aim to schedule shorter meetings that are timed to meet the objectives, not arbitrarily set.*** As most of us use digital calendars, such as Outlook, when we schedule a meeting it is ordinarily set to schedule in 30-minute increments. You will therefore find that most meetings are set in those increments, when the proper scheduling of

the meeting could mean that a meeting of, for example, 20, 45 or 70 minutes would be more appropriate.

4. ***Set clear objectives and expectations for the outcome and participation of the meeting.*** What do you expect from each attendee's participation? How will they contribute to the meeting's effectiveness in delivering its objectives? Do they know what the expectations on them are and are they willing and able to meet them?

   Through the lens of BTFA, this also links to the neuroscience behind goal setting, making progress, and the positive effect of dopamine (as part of the reward system) on the brain. This makes it crucial for motivation, energy, ownership, autonomous teams and other terms often associated with the 'HR' function.

5. ***Send pre-read or preparation materials in advance – normally around two working days ahead.*** All of the participants must be well prepared for the meeting or it won't be effective. In the check-in, ensure that everyone is prepared and even consider postponing if people are not. It can send a strong message, and also set the scene for future meetings, if you have the courage to delay the meeting if the participants cannot participate fully. An alternative is to schedule reading time into the beginning of the meeting, providing people with the time to read the preparation materials before the meeting begins in full.

6. ***Start and end on time.*** Showing respect for people's time will ultimately be reciprocated as, if you can demonstrate to people that your meetings always begin and end on time, they will start showing up on time, as they know that they will not be kept waiting and will be able to get to their next appointments on time. This links well with countermeasure #3 and can be augmented by beginning meetings at five minutes past the hour (or half hour) and ending them at least five minutes before the next period increment. This will provide people with a real incentive to be on time but takes quite a bit of discipline from you as the facilitator of the meeting.

7. ***Avoid monologues, be brief and engage all participants.*** Whilst participants must have sufficient time to contribute, it is important that they don't spend time in long explanations or justifications, and instead the dialogue should be focussed on the purpose of the meeting and the data brought to it. More detailed input to the meeting should be provided ahead of the meeting as pre-read.

8. ***Stay focussed, moving tangential discussions to off-line discussions or an alternative meeting.*** Linked to countermeasure #6, if any of the participants bring in opinions or wish to discuss tangential items, these should be captured as actions for follow-up and not be allowed to consume the meeting. In the event that something is brought up that fundamentally changes the proposition of the meeting, such as an expert opinion that is countering the current data, then a decision will have to be made whether the meeting must be postponed pending follow-up action, rather than having an opinion-based discussion.

9. ***Capture decisions and actions, with a single owner and due date, and distribute after the meeting.*** A decision and action log is an important tool for an effective meeting. As decisions are made, or actions assigned, they should be captured, confirming with the group that the decision is recognised by all, or that the action owner agrees with the action as worded and its due date is realistic. The action owner should be a single person, even where multiple people will participate, as it is crucial that one person feels true ownership to deliver it. The owner should, of course, be someone present in the meeting, even if they might engage with others who were not part of the meeting.

10. ***Follow-up on actions to their completion.*** It is crucial for the integrity of the meeting that all actions are followed up on to their satisfactory conclusion. Where the meeting is a recurring one, the first element after check-in should be an action review, to ensure that all committed actions have been completed on time or are on track to do so. Where the meeting was a one-off, the meeting owner must follow up with action owners and, if there are issues, reconvene to review and problem solve any under-delivery.

The TOR is a very simple, but highly effective, document that ensures that the person chairing the meeting has considered the most important aspects of the meeting:

1. When will the meeting be, how long is required, is it recurring or a one-off, where will it be held, is it virtual or in-person?
2. What type of meeting is it? Is it one focussed on growing the business, its governance or problem solving? Obviously, we want to be working on the first type as much as possible, use governance meetings

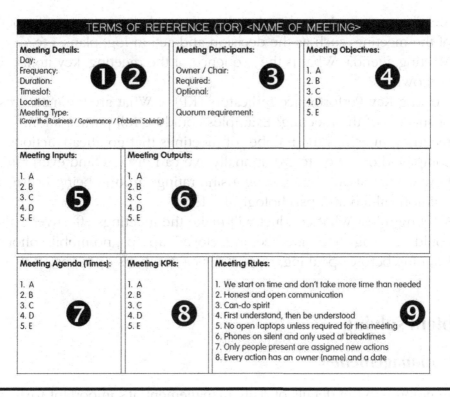

Figure 4.2 A Terms of Reference (TOR) example

sparingly but sufficiently to maintain effectiveness, and aim to turn most of our problem solving into grow the business activity (proactive problem solving for strategic and improvement activity), minimising the amount of time problem solving failures.

3. Meeting participants: Who should be there, who can be optionally there (only applicable for induction, knowledge sharing or learning opportunities), and what attendance makes a quorum? This last aspect is critical, as the meeting outcome requires some decisions to be made, or actions to be taken, and therefore we need to ensure that the people attending are empowered to make those decisions. If someone necessary to endorse any decisions made is not in attendance, then the meeting shouldn't proceed.

4. Meeting objectives: What should be achieved at the end of the meeting? What will success look like as an outcome?

5. Meeting inputs: What inputs are required for the meeting to go ahead? Is data required? Pre-reads, previous outcomes of meetings, prior decisions?

6. Meeting outputs: Linked to the objectives, what are the specific outputs of the meeting, such as the decision and action log, plans, etc.?
7. Meeting agenda: What is the sequence of the meeting, key items, times and owners?
8. Meeting Key Performance Indicators (KPIs): What are the measures of success of the meeting? Examples could be full participation, for recurring meetings the number of meetings that go ahead, actions completed on time etc. Additionally, we can discuss, and even rate, how we felt about the meeting, using ratings around being heard, opinion valued and psychological safety.
9. Meeting rules: What conduct will make the meetings effective? This could be things like time-keeping, closed laptops, no mobile phones, listening before speaking, respect for each other's opinions, etc.

Problem solving

Daily management

Before going into the details of daily management, it's important to answer a question that one of the readers of my draft manuscript asked, and I'm sure many others might wonder. He asked me why a section called problem solving first covered daily management and leader standard work before problem solving.

I smile when I'm asked this question, as I've encountered this many times. In my current company, GKN Aerospace, as we deployed our Lean operating model most of our practitioners asked why the module on problem solving was actually a combined daily management and problem-solving activity. We discussed it and tried to intellectually resolve the disagreement on doing it like this, but couldn't come to a conclusion, as I found it difficult to gain the belief in its validity. However, after a few months of deployment, where the initial rigour around first putting the daily management in place wasn't always present, the belief started to grow as the BTFA and PDCA cycles ran in parallel. Today, the consensus is firmly that we must put daily management in place first, because without it we aren't clear on what the problems really are, and we can't properly problem solve as we don't have adequate and reliable data to do so.

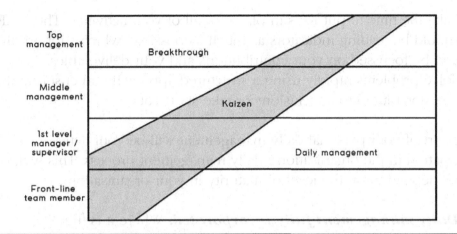

Figure 4.3   Daily management for Lean leadership

I covered daily management extensively in *The Simplicity of Lean* but it's really important that we remember that this is not about the tool of daily management but rather how you apply this to your way of working, or more accurately your way of thinking about daily management, ensuring that you manage your activity in alignment with its philosophy.

To emphasise this more deeply, let's start with the tenets of daily management, its raison d'être if you will, which are:

1. Short interval control (SIC)
2. A focus on key performance indicators (KPIs)
3. Rapid problem solving

Dependent upon your position in the organisation, you will spend more or less time on daily management activity, as the Daily Management for Lean Leadership diagram illustrates. Your management of the breakthrough, Kaizen and daily management activities will be through the use of the personal Kanban and the execution of effective daily management activity will provide you with the 'oxygen' to focus on the breakthrough and Kaizen activities.

The approach that I propose is:

1. Establish your leader standard work so that it's clear what you must do on a daily, weekly, monthly and quarterly basis.
2. Put in place SIC to ensure that you can discover, as soon as possible, when you are off-track. The personal Kanban will support you in this, guiding you to schedule activity on time and highlighting, rapidly, when you are behind schedule.

3. Take the time to put KPIs in place for all of your activities. These KPIs should be leading indicators as much as possible, which support SIC, and be focussed on your contributions and your deliverables.
4. Solve problems rapidly using a structured approach and ensuring that you don't jump to conclusions or take short cuts.

A big part of your personal daily management will be your active participation in the organisation's daily management process. This will, of course, depend upon the level of maturity in your organisation:

■ ***Daily management fully incorporated:*** Where it is fully integrated into the organisation, you will probably already be actively participating. However, in this case you must ask yourself whether you are personally living it in managing your own commitments or are simply a passenger in the organisation's use of it.
■ ***Daily management partially in use or in its infancy:*** In a scenario in which it is partially in place, or in its infancy, this provides you with the opportunity to take a leadership role in its success, as you can live it in your personal activity, which will shine through as you participate, and help to grow, the organisation's process.
■ ***Daily management not in place:*** This is also a fantastic opportunity to take a leadership position and demonstrate role-model behaviour, not only by expecting everyone in the organisation to participate but by demonstrating your activism in it.

I often hear the challenge from people that daily management isn't possible for their type of work, that they have a much longer cycle of activity or lead-time to completion. However, my response is that what they do still requires daily activity and that, by clearly defining what must happen successfully every day in order to deliver the total outcome, they can avoid the overload peaks that normally happen towards the end of the cycle. I would actually argue that it is even more important in the case of product development, financial processes, long-cycle manufacturing, or the like, where delays, quality issues, or cost over-runs are traditionally discovered long after their root cause has occurred. This is the contradiction of daily management, that it is typically implemented in those areas for which it is easiest to do so, and neglected for the more challenging, but arguably more necessary, processes.

I can assure you that if you sincerely utilise daily management for a period of time, you'll see the uptick in your performance as you become more effective in what you do.

Leader standard work

Leader standard work is a visual daily management system for all levels of leadership in the organisation, starting from the team leader level through to the CEO. It is intended to ensure that a significant proportion of daily tasks are executed in a systematic and standardised manner, resulting in a predictability that benefits the organisation's stability and its operational excellence. However, it must be noted that by using the term predictability, I am not implying that the leaders do not challenge the organisation. In fact, Lean leaders are constantly challenging the organisation but, crucially, they do this in a way that tests the organisation's capability to achieve operational excellence and not by constantly surprising the organisation with new direction, ideas or priorities.

Leader standard work consists of three core elements:

1. It is visual in nature.
2. It is undertaken on a regular cadence.
3. It drives both action and learning.

Leader standard work is often resisted by managers, particularly at the upper level of the hierarchy. This is sometimes due to the misconception that they cannot standardise what they do; a view that what managers or executives do is something of an 'art form'. Alternatively, it can be that they view standardising what they do as in some way devaluing their importance in the organisation; a status-driven mind-set whereby the person in question believes that they are too important to be 'told' what to do on a regular basis.

It is correct that the level (or degree) of standardisation for a manager will be lower than that of a shop-floor worker, as there are more requirements upon them for flexibility in their agenda. Nevertheless, the standardisation of a good part of their daily activities will ensure that the leader provides a predictability that offers their people the stability to get their daily management activities done, problem solve and deliver customer value. As Figure 4.4 demonstrates, we would expect that an operator has

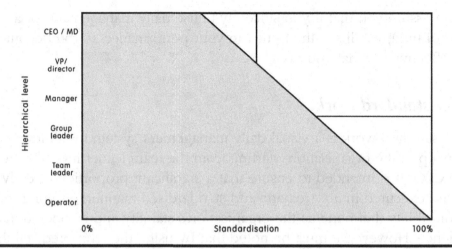

Figure 4.4   Levels of standardisation throughout the hierarchy

virtually all of their daily work standardised, which will be the normal value-added tasks of their job plus their Kaizen activities. Their team leader might have a little more flexibility in their scheduled activities, as they will need to react to 'non-standard' activities, problems etc. and so will typically have 10–20% of their time that is not standardised. As you can see, the level of non-standard activity in this model increases until we reach the CEO level, at which the standardised time is around 40% of their day.

However, as the organisation moves along the maturity curve, I firmly believe that the curve can be moved to the right, as more of the daily tasks may be standardised when the organisational stability is increased. This is a virtuous cycle, as the increased stability brought about through daily management, problem solving and standardised work delivers more opportunity to standardise, which in turn allows for more stability of performance. As I mentioned in the personal Kanban section earlier, despite being at the level of the organisation that the model would suggest has 40–50% standardisation, I've developed it up to a level of around 70% of my activities, as I've been able to standardise the processes by which I create breakthrough and Kaizen. This happened as my belief in leader standard work increased, I experienced and thought about the benefits that I was deriving from its use, and felt its positivity.

The leader standard work must deliver three things to be successful:

1. Document the current state of your best practices.
2. Create the baseline for your future improvement.

Lean Master & Expert Leader Standard Work

				Standard Tasks By Frequency								
Weekly	T.O.R. Or Std. Work	Std. Time	Notes	Monthly	T.O.R. Or Std. Work	Std. Time	Notes	Quarterly	T.O.R. Or Std. Work	Std. Time	Notes
Meetings:											
Daily Management Meeting	85.1.31	1		Hoshin Meeting	85.1.27	2		Submit Philips Mindsets & Behaviour Nomination		0.25	
Event preparation calls	N/A	1		Performance Review with the Head of Continuous Improvement	84.1.09	0.5		Run PC maintenance program		1	
Deployment meetings/calls with Site Lean Champions:				Development Review with the Head of Continuous Improvement	84.1.10	0.5		Back up files on PC		1	
<Site 1>	85.1.01	0.5		Material Management Meeting	85.1.08	1					
<Site 2>	85.1.01	0.5		Perform office 6S including SharePoint Zone Kamishibai	N/A	0.5					
<Site 3>	85.1.01	0.5		Prepare and attend CI Circle meeting	85.1.13	1					
<Site 4>	85.1.01	0.5		Perform team member kamishibai		0.5					
Meeting Preparation:											
Update the Daily Management Board	N/A	0.25		Prepare and upload golden moments to SharePoint prior to the MMM	N/A	0.5					
Update Hoshin file	N/A	0.5		Review and update the team ILU	N/A	0.25					
Ensure that A3s are updated and uploaded to SharePoint and update the A3 tracker	N/A	0.1		Update the personal KPI tracker ahead of the monthly performance review	N/A	0.5					
Review and update Team action tracker	N/A	0.25		Update the action tracker for the personal development actions	N/A	0.25					
Ensure that the site storyboards are uploaded to SharePoint	N/A	0.1									
Event Planning, Execution & Follow up:											
Follow deployment management standard work	86.0.01										
Update the team planning file on SharePoint for the next 4 weeks.	N/A	0.25		Review and raise Kaizen for Lean Master/ Lean Expert LSW	85.1.19	0.25					
Review the work life balance using the standard on the second worksheet	N/A	0.25		Prepare for Sprint Weeks	85.1.29	3					
Book any travel for confirmed events at least 2 weeks in advance	N/A	0.5									
Review Outlook calendar for the coming week and reschedule meetings if they clash with travel plans	N/A	0.5									
Update NPS Scores and Event on time (in EPF)	N/A	0.25									
Submit travel expenses in Concur	N/A	0.5									
Update the travel budget file	N/A	0.1									
Update the Lean Consultancy Revenue Model	N/A	0.1									
Update the Cross Sector Calibration file	N/A	0.1									
Post any updates to the Continuous Improvement ConnextUs site	N/A	1									
Raise kaizen for Deployment	99.0.5	0.5									
Raise One Point Lessons for Deployment	N/A	0.5									
Other Tasks:											
Implement material updates assigned to Lean Master/ Expert	N/A	0.5		Be in Amsterdam or Singapore during home office weeks			On hold due to travel restrictions	Attend internal & external lean events to expand knowledge and network	N/A	4	
Read posts on ConnectUs	N/A	1						Expand the Kaikaku network by visiting new companies and interacting with other lean network groups	N/A	4	
6S for Office: Review your 6S (physical & virtual) and follow the Sweep routine	ODM 2.5.6	0.25		6S for Office: Conduct 6S Audit (physical & virtual)	ODM 2.6.6	0.5		Update the Kaikaku Network with new information	N/A	0.25	
Other Tasks When On-Site											
				Attend Site Steering Team Meeting	N/A	1					
				Check 1 Standard Work item per Site	N/A	0.5					
				Gemba Walk	N/A	1					
				Check the 25 week plan & 100 week vision	N/A	0.5					
				Check the communication plan	N/A	0.5					
				Review the bottoms up kaizens from yesterday	N/A	0.25					
				Attend the daily kaizen report outs	N/A	1					
				Review the site storyboard and outstanding actions towards Phase Gate Exit	N/A	0.5					
				Review ILU of key Lean site deployment team members	N/A	0.25					
Standard Time for Weekly Tasks		11.5		**Standard Time for Monthly Tasks**		11.25		**Standard Time for Quarterly Tasks**		10.5	
% of time per month that is standardised		38%		**Standard Time for Monthly Tasks On-Site**		8.5					

Figure 4.5   A leader standard work template

3. Define your expected behaviours.

Like most of the Lean tools, it isn't complicated to populate or use but it's the discipline to follow your leader standard work that will be your main challenge, especially when you're under pressure.

Problem solving

Problem solving is a large subject and is covered in detail in *The Simplicity of Lean*. The focus in *Living Lean* is around how you can adopt it into how you practise your work on a daily basis, and make it a success for you. As you run your daily management, based upon your leader standard work, ensuring that you are doing this with the maximum personal effectiveness, you'll encounter problems. The way that you deal with those problems will be the difference between the success and failure of your new modus operandi.

Many people work on 'gut feel' or experience, especially those who have a long tenure in their field and have experienced what they perceive to be the same problems before. The skill and experience of people is a crucial part of problem solving but the danger is that this becomes the exclusive approach and provides a perception of saving time through the avoidance of the bureaucracy of formal and structured problem solving, the avoidance of running PDCA in its entirety. This also links to the acceptance of problems, whereby the experience of the participants can actually blind them to the real problem and its root causes, as they take short-cuts, or make assumptions, accepting the chronic problems as 'normal'.

Challenging the degree to which structure versus intuition leads to the desired outcomes is a significant BTFA issue, with the alignment of action necessarily requiring an alignment of beliefs. If a deep alignment is missing, then there will be emotional tensions in teams, which remain hidden due to a lack of psychological safety. It is the Lean leader's responsibility to help to develop the environment by which team members feel safe to make problems visible and to challenge assumptions. Leaders and other experienced team members, who can easily use their experience and 'gut feel' can stifle this, as they overwhelm other team members as they justify their own opinions and impose a process on people who are not psychologically able to accept it.

As shown in Figure 4.6, typically the reduction in the planning and check part of problem solving, moving more to a Do and Act approach, takes much more time than following the PDCA process in full, positively using the experience and skills of experienced team members to more

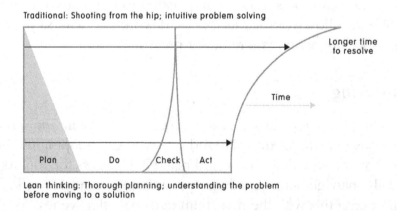

Figure 4.6 Time consumption in a traditional vs Lean thinking approach to problem solving

thoroughly plan and implement the countermeasures. This will be a true BTFA process, as the experienced team members will have strong beliefs in their knowledge of what needs to be done, and will feel aggrieved at having to 'waste time' to undertake thorough problem solving, and *Living Lean* will involve working to demonstrate the advantages and superior outcomes of the comprehensive approach.

For most of us, there are two key problem-solving tools that we ought to practise to support our daily activities:

1. 3C problem solving
2. A3 problem solving

3C problem solving

This is the basic problem-solving methodology and the one that you will be using most regularly. When practised well and often it will soon become second nature and is the core driver of Kaizen.

The 3Cs stand for Concern, Cause and Countermeasure and the way that they are used are that you will identify a concern related to performance and rapidly determine the actual problem statement, determining how big a problem it is. Where it is a low priority, you might decide to take no current action, whereas if it is a moderate problem it may be that you decide to take some immediate action, although perhaps you don't get to the root cause and instead implement a rapid countermeasure that only addresses the symptoms, and doesn't necessarily address the root cause. However, where the problem is a clear and present issue, you will address it rapidly. Safety issues, of course, fall into the latter category.

3C problem solving is great in enabling you to rapidly prioritise and solve, either on a short-term symptom-based level or root-cause basis, the majority of your daily issues. Hopefully you can see how it still harnesses your

Concern	Cause	Countermeasure	Owner	Due date	Status
Daily Sales with Customer X below target for 3 consecutive Days	'Rapid Quotes' not being sent within the agreed lead-time - No-one fully certified to undertake it, causing slow response times.	Short-Term: Team Leader to provide rapid training intervention and to support the quotations process for the next 5 working days. Long-Term: Open an A3 to understand how the competence deficiency was not spotted and why this critical process is not a priority induction item.	Paul Smith	04/03/2018	C

Figure 4.7   An example of a 3C

experience and skills but also uses a clear framework that helps you to stay disciplined in really thinking through your problem statement, the cause of the concern and the right countermeasure. A symptom of a lack of belief or understanding of the process is where the concern and countermeasure have been completed but the cause is either blank or has scant information in it. It demonstrates a propensity to jump to conclusions and to not take the time to really understand what the cause was. It takes a lot of energy to coach and convince team members to do it correctly, and the 'knack point' of this is to demonstrate the improved problem-solving efficacy and hence the why.

A3 problem solving

All problem solving should begin with 3C problem solving but, where it is clear that more thorough investigation and analysis are required, A3 problem solving supports this.

The A3 is a format that supports you in following the eight steps of problem solving, which is a more sophisticated methodology for ensuring that true root-cause analysis is undertaken in the problem solving.

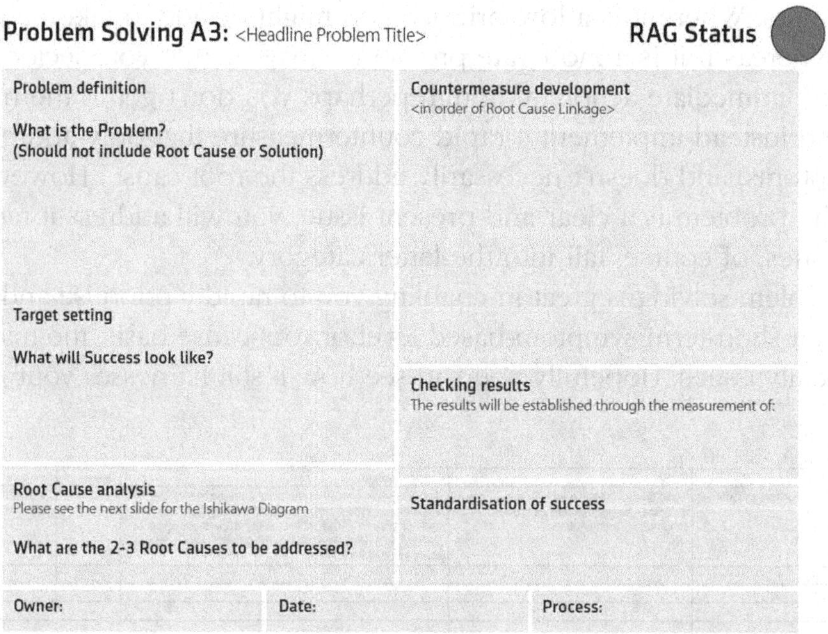

Figure 4.8   The A3 problem-solving document

As we run through the problem-solving process, it can be very useful to have a 'vehicle' to collate and communicate with, and the beauty of the A3 document is that it naturally guides you through the eight-step process. The document gets its name from the fact that, pre-email, the largest document that could easily be sent by a fax machine was an A3-size piece of paper (roughly equivalent to the American 11-inch by 17-inch tabloid-sized paper). 'A3s' are used in Toyota to communicate Problem Solving, Status, and Proposals, with the idea being that lengthy documents should not be required to build consensus and agreement if clarity of thought is evident. This doesn't mean that background documents are not available and technical analyses, Ishikawa documents, reports, etc. will exist 'behind' the A3. However, the A3 itself is the focal point of discussion amongst the team. The eight steps of problem solving are as follows:

Clarify the problem

To be successful in problem solving, you must ensure that it is stated clearly, fact based and aligned amongst all stakeholders. The best method for this is to use the 5W + 1H approach:

What is the problem? – Describe what is observable.

Why is it a problem? – Explain what the negative effect is.

Where is it a problem? – Identify where the problem is emanating from or is observable.

When is it a problem? – Provide details of when the problem occurs or is observable.

Who is it a problem for? – Who is affected? This could well be directly impacting the customer but is also likely to be impacting people within the organisation.

How much of a problem is it? – What data do you have to demonstrate the size of the problem?

Break down the problem

Once you've determined the problem statement and decided that you ought to proceed with solving it, you must determine whether you can solve this problem as a single issue, or whether it makes sense to break it down into smaller, more manageable problems, which you can then either prioritise and tackle one-by-one, or delegate to others.

Set a target

Once you have the baseline of the problem, you must determine what the target is that you're aiming for. Sometimes that will be determined by necessity, whilst in other circumstances it could be that you have desired targets, which are more about improvement than a short-term absolute business requirement. In terms of setting the target, it's important to ensure that you set a clearly measurable target that is a true performance outcome. What you shouldn't do is confuse the target with what you will do (the achievement of actions).

Analyse the root cause

In this step, you must get to the underlying root cause. It is imperative that the problem be analysed to get to root cause, with the most effective approach being:

■ Go to the Gemba (the place where the work is done) and identify all potential causes (assumptions).
■ Categorise and display possible root causes (prioritise).
■ Gather data to determine the root cause (analyse).

A powerful tool for going through this process is the Ishikawa, or fishbone, diagram, which stimulates the team's thinking around the possible causes, in a visual manner. The team use the listed categories to group the possible causes. Once populated, you can then prioritise the most likely culprits, before moving into the 5 x why analysis to get them to the root cause.

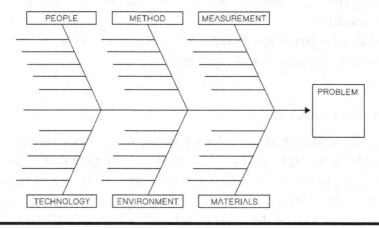

Figure 4.9   An example of an Ishikawa diagram

Develop countermeasures

Once you understand the root cause(s), you can determine and develop countermeasures. Both short-term and long-term countermeasures should be considered, as sometimes the urgency of solving the problem will mean that measures are required that, whilst not desirable in the long term, are necessary to alleviate the immediate need.

In reality, even though there is a certain simplicity in visualising the eight steps in a logical PDCA flow, as the diagram shows on the right-hand side, the problem solving team will, in reality, be going through rapid PDCA–BTFA cycles throughout the eight steps.

See countermeasures through

Countermeasures must be rapidly implemented, one-by-one, and the learning achieved. The PDCA wheel is rapidly turning at this point, and this is the stage in which the hard work done in planning the countermeasures will either come to fruition or be wasted.

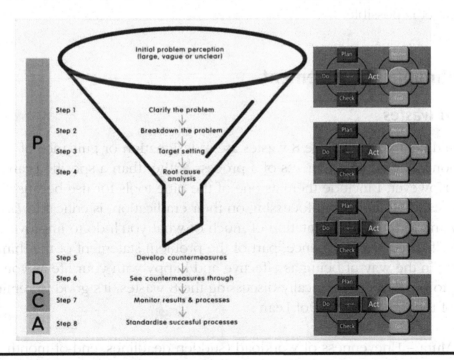

Figure 4.10   The 8-step problem-solving process

Evaluate both results and process

The implementation of the countermeasures is not the end of your work, as you had set targets and must ensure that the countermeasures have delivered what you intended them to deliver.

You must check both the results and the process: (Results) Did you reach the target condition? (Process) Was the countermeasure effective or did you get lucky? Was your hypothesis correct? What worked well, what didn't? Where did you deviate from the plan? What did you learn from this? What could you do better next time? Could you do it more quickly next time?

Standardise success, adapt, or restart if unsuccessful

If you have been successful, you must 'lock-in' the success by defining the new standard, underpinning the success by making it your new way of working. You must also ensure that you share your learning across the organisation, looking for other similar problems that could benefit from this solution.

If you have been unsuccessful, either fully or partially, it's important that you understand why, use that learning, and restart the PDCA cycle. It is highly unlikely that, if you've followed this structured approach with rigour and discipline, you will experience total failure, but some level of missing the target is possible.

Continuous improvement

The 8 wastes

It could be argued that the 8 wastes are a designation or guidance of the non-value-added elements of a process, rather than a specific Lean tool. However, I include them as one of the nine tools for use because understanding them, and focussing on their eradication, is critical to *Living Lean* and to the implementation of much of what you'll do to improve yourself. They are, in essence, part of the problem statement of the things getting in the way of being as effective and happy with your life as you want to be. Before specifically discussing the 8 wastes, it's good to remind you of the three 'enemies of Lean':

- Mura – Unevenness of workload (sudden deadlines, end-of-month orders, month-end closing, etc.)

- Muri – Overburden of workload (an unequal distribution of work across team members, 'fire-fighting' activity, stress and burn-out)
- Muda – Waste in the work, which gets in the way of delivering value to the customers (the 8 wastes)

The tools covered in this chapter are intended to help you in tackling these three enemies of Lean, as you balance your workload with tools such as personal Kanban, reduce the over-burden with tools such as time management, use problem-solving tools to tackle the waste, and then use the continuous improvement tools to make your ways-of-working better every day. As introduced in *Leading with Lean*, TIM WOODS is the acronym that I have adopted as the mnemonic for the 8 wastes. These 8 wastes are:

Transportation

This is any activity where materials, product, information, or service is moved around. Whilst it is intrinsically necessary to transport items or information, we must reduce this as much as possible.

> *Ask yourself: Do the processes that you're involved in transport information or products more often than is absolutely necessary?*

Inventory

Wherever there is the creation of a stock of goods, data, people, etc. it is considered inventory. Whilst some level of inventory is necessary to facilitate a smooth operation and prevent delays and stoppages, its minimisation is essential to the effective creation of flow, where problems are quickly visible. I often consider inventory to be the worst of the wastes, as it accumulates all of the others into an expensive cost burden on the organisation.

> *Ask yourself: Do the processes that you're involved in create excessive inventory? In non-manufacturing processes, are too many projects started but not completed, applications left awaiting approval, for example?*

Motion

Motion is where the activity of a person happens, such as moving between stations, walking to a photo-copier, etc. Motion is distinct in that it refers to the team members, whereas transportation refers to the materials, products and information moving.

> *Ask yourself: Do the processes that you're involved in involve too much movement? Motion in these processes isn't great aerobic exercise and so don't worry about reducing your steps. Instead, remove the motion waste and then use the time saving to do some real exercise!*

Waiting

This waste refers to the time that a step in the process is awaiting an input or to deliver an output. It is generally wasteful, as it is unproductive time and means that flow has broken down. However, I often consider this the least bad waste, simply because if we're waiting, we're not creating the much more wasteful elements of over-production, defects or inventory. Therefore waiting should be viewed as wasteful when it is due to a poorly running process but not when our team members have stopped to solve a problem.

> *Ask yourself: Is there a lot of waiting time in your work day? Could you synchronise your work with others better using some of the Living Lean tools?*

Over-production

Over-production is one of the most common wastes in a traditional organisation, as the historic mind-set of mass production, economies of scale, sweat the assets and the people, and the general reluctance to 'stop and fix' problems, means that more of the product, information or service is created than is needed.

> *Ask yourself: Do you labour under the efficiency fallacy, working, working, working, when perhaps a step needs to be taken back to assess whether the work being done really meets the needs of the customer?*

Over-processing

Not to be confused with over-production, this is when too much activity is undertaken to create the outcome, whether it is milling too much material from a part, over-cleaning the product or asking for too many approval signatures. Essentially, it is activity in the process that is more than is sensibly required to deliver a great product or service.

> *Ask yourself: Are there too many discussions, ineffective problem solving, revisiting of decisions, and opinion-based debate in your daily work?*

Defects

These are any quality issue with the product or service, not only at the point of delivery to the final customer, but at any stage in the process. Often quality is viewed as the final outcome, but in Lean terms it is understood that the quality that the end customer receives is the accumulation of the quality at every step in the value stream. Defects must be eradicated at every step, not simply tackled at the end.

> *Ask yourself: Do you have the right mind-set for quality? Do you consider zero defects part of your responsibility and ensure that you don't accept poor quality, nor pass it on?*

Skills (their under-utilisation)

The previous 7 wastes are the traditional wastes of Lean thinking. However, in more recent times skills, or more precisely their under-utilisation, was added. This is by far the most wasteful of them all, as our people are the only productive asset that appreciates, and human beings have an inherent array of knowledge, skills and attributes that may be utilised by an organisation. Lean organisations understand this and partner with their team members to make every day a beneficial set of activities for both the company and its people. Where an organisation wastes its people's talent, it wastes its biggest opportunities for success.

> *Ask yourself: Is the first part of anything you do focussed on the impact on people and how you can engage colleagues and team members in an effective outcome?*

Kaizen everyday

We all want to make a big impact on our organisation's performance, don't we? It's a part of being human that we want recognition for the work that we do and what we've achieved and, in a traditional organisation, it's often only the 'big things' that are readily recognised.

Sometimes it can even be the case that recognition is given to team members or individuals for fixing a big problem that was causing significant issues for the organisation, where the irony is that they were the very team or individuals who were responsible for the issue in the first place. It might seem uncharitable to raise this as an issue, as many times it's absolutely necessary to undertake this kind of 'fire-fighting', and people spend a lot of time and effort to do so. However, it's equally important that we recognise those teams and individuals who are, by *Living Lean*, ensuring that the problems are avoided in the first place.

Kaizen everyday is a highly effective way for you to do this, which, simply put, means that when you encounter a problem, no matter how small, you quickly problem solve, most of the time using 3C problem solving, but most importantly then 'lock-in' the countermeasure by making an update to the standard for that activity. That is a Kaizen, the improvement of a standard based upon problem solving. This is what I call the art of improvement, having the mind-set that every little grain of improvement will contribute to a larger, cumulative impact on the organisation. It doesn't need to be significant in itself, in fact that's the beauty of it, that it is quick and easy to implement and, when each and every team member implements a number of them per year, the organisation improves far more than any project team could have achieved on its own. That's not to say that we don't need step change improvement; quite the contrary, we need both, but the frequency and quantity of Kaizen will be much greater.

Kaizen are not simply good ideas, but rather they are the outcome of solving one of the three types of problem:

1. The standard is not achieved
2. The standard is achieved but with high variation
3. The current standard is achieved but a new standard is required

The Kaizen process is therefore to run to standard, expose a problem where one exists, use the problem-solving process to implement a

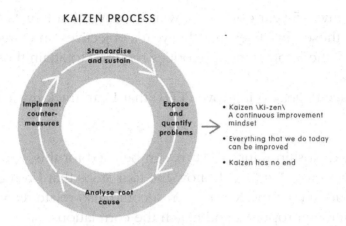

Figure 4.11 The Kaizen process

countermeasure but then, most importantly, to ensure that it is sustainably implemented through an update to the standard. Where a standard didn't formally exist, as it was unwritten or maintained in an informal manner, it should be created.

A really important aspect of Kaizen is that it is about looking inwards, avoiding the very human approach of looking at others to improve; we could do things really well if only others would change or if the systems were upgraded or fixed. However, we are much more the masters of our own destiny than we recognise, and we must therefore rid ourselves of excuses and prevarication, and instead focus on action and Kaizen.

Personal Hoshin (Kanri)

Personal Hoshin is the practice of applying Hoshin Kanri on your personal goals. Within a Lean organisation Hoshin Kanri will be a core process and translate the organisation's strategy into action. From this each area of the business will be clear on how it contributes to the breakthrough activity, and this will translate into each employee's personal objectives.

However, it can be taken a little further and I personally apply it for both my personal and professional objectives to ensure that any breakthroughs that I want to make are clearly focussed and ultimately have the best chance of success.

The way that I do this is similar to the process that would be taken for an organisation and goes as follows:

1. Establish my 3–5-year objectives, with improvement targets.
2. Translate those objectives into this year's objectives and targets.
3. Determine the improvement priorities required to attain those objectives.
4. Put in place targets to improve (TTIs) that I can track my achievement against.

The standard Hoshin Kanri X-Matrix can be used for this, and you can see on the diagram in Figure 4.12 how the four steps that I run through link to the four quadrants of the X-Matrix. You could also relate resources that you need, where appropriate, and match the correlations.

Whether or not you want to go to this extent is entirely up to you. I don't normally and usually establish it in a simple spreadsheet. However, I did for this last one, prompted specifically by writing this book and wanting to try it out in anticipation, and I found it to be useful, as it seemed to somehow, intangibly, help me to internalise the commitment that I was making. Perhaps this is related to the BTFA cycle so, whilst my logical brain might say that it is overkill to create the X-Matrix for a personal Hoshin, maybe the emotional acceptance of the changes that I wanted to make

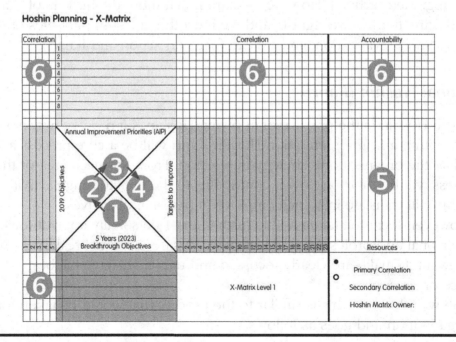

Figure 4.12 The Hoshin Kanri X-Matrix

are helped by going through the process and helped me to foster my commitment?

It is when leaders consciously lead others to the destination (wisdom) which they themselves have benefited from that a Lean culture emerges. People are in the right place in their heads (BTFA) to enjoy innovative thinking, which can all inform 'profit-share' decisions and other choices leaders make to create a high-performance culture.

Later on in the book I'll show you the specific examples for the writing of this book and reaching my fitness targets, and how I combined that with daily management to achieve the desired outcome.

Hansei

Before moving onto the next chapter, please take a few moments to reflect and consider what, in relation to your own way of working and actions, are:

Your key learning points?

The changes that you could make?

Current problems that they would help to solve?

Note

1 How Much Time Do We Spend in Meetings? (Hint: It's Scary), The Muse. (www.themuse.com/advice/how-much-time-do-we-spend-in-meetings-hint-its-scary)

HANDS

II

Chapter 5

Practising Lean

Using the tools

As you begin *Living Lean*, you will be practising using the tools that
I discussed in the previous chapter. Remember, the premise of the book
is that, even if you practise the tools *on your organisation*, the only way
to become a true Lean leader is to practise them *on yourself* and the way
that you manage your own ways-of-working. A good example of this is the
8 wastes, and how you can utilise their reduction to make yourself more
effective in your work, at the same time improving your life balance.

The 8 wastes are assessed in terms of how they impede the creation
of customer value, which could be the end customer of your business or
organisation, or the next step in your process, which might be a colleague
who receives input from your activity. However, in terms of *Living Lean*
this might also be your family, friends, community or yourself, in terms of
whether the waste is causing you to work excessively and being unable to
devote sufficient time to them.

Compare our attitude to working additional time in industry versus
sports. In industry, taking extra time or working long hours is often
celebrated as commitment, whereas in sports it's clearly seen as a
failure: The sprinter who takes 15 seconds to run 100 m is not the one on
the podium, a five-set tennis match at Wimbledon is great to watch but not
generally the target of the tennis players. However, the team member who
spends 60+ hours to do their job, whilst contracted at 40 hours, is seen as

DOI: 10.4324/9781003251385-7

highly committed and to be recognised, rather than asking why they need to work an additional 50% of the 'standard' hours for their job.

Think about this simple example:

Standard / contracted working hours per week: 40 hours
Normal working hours per week: 52 hours
Additional working hours per week: 12 hours

We might often consider that this is what is needed to get the job done and simply accept it. However, consider the situation as follows:

Budgeted project expenditure per week: $40,000
Actual project expenditure per week: $52,000
Additional project expenditure per week: $12,000

How long do you think that this second scenario would be tolerated? Not for very long, of course, and there would be a significant effort to solve the issue and get back to budget. The over-budget spend would be considered a failure and unacceptable, as tangible hard cash would be leaving the business unnecessarily.

Nonetheless, the first scenario is perhaps even more than tolerated; it is accepted as the norm and those people who are able to work within their standard hours are somehow considered uncommitted, whilst those working the long hours (and of course the 52-hours example is not exceptional) are to some extent the corporate heroes. However, the fundamental issue is that, where additional time is being put in, it should be due to a real current need to work those hours to get the job done, an exception, not simply due to waste in the working practices and a structural, continuing situation.

What can start to help in our thinking about this is when we consider the fact that the value-added portion of the work that we do will typically be less than 10%. This means that the amount of time per hour that you will add value is 6 minutes. The calculation for scenario 1 therefore expands to become:

Standard / contracted working value-added hours per week: 4 hours
  (240 minutes)
Normal working value-added hours per week: 5.2 hours (312 minutes)
Additional working value-added hours per week: 1.2 hours (72 minutes)

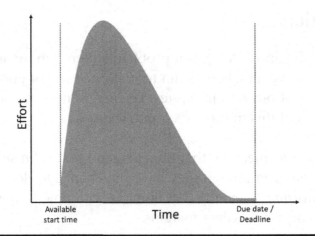

Figure 5.1   Parkinson's Law

This means that you could potentially spend an additional 12 hours per week away from other activities (family, friends, sports, community, yourself) to add an extra 72 minutes of value! Therefore, the alternative is to reduce the waste in the standard / contractual hours to create the additional value-added time, which in this example requires a 3% absolute value-added improvement:

> *Standard / contracted working value-added hours per week (10% of 40 hours): 4 hours improvement of 3% value-added hours per week (13% of 40 hours): 5.2 hours*
> *Additional working value-added hours per week: 1.2 hours*

Rather than working an extra 12 hours per week, reducing the waste in what you do by 3.3% (90% waste reduced to 87%) would provide the same amount of value add for your organisation's customers (1.2 hours) whilst increasing the value add for your personal customers by a whopping 12 hours. That is surely food for thought and an opportunity to get more of what you really want to do done, and is a great example of using the tools on yourself as well as on the organisation.

It is therefore really important that you practise the use of the Lean tools on yourself and understand how they work for you, which will allow you to discover what you can achieve from their utilisation. I'll talk later in the book about what you'll experience as you feel and begin to believe, but none of that is possible unless you practise. As the old saying goes, *practise makes perfect!*

Procrastination

Procrastination, the art of delay, is a problem suffered more acutely by some, although we've all fallen victim to it at one time or another and it is the waiting waste of our 8 Lean wastes. Lechler, Ronen and Stohr addressed two key elements of this in their 2005 publication[1]:

- *Parkinson's Law*, meaning that humans tend not to finish their tasks ahead of time even though they have the chance to do so.
- *Student syndrome*, meaning that humans with time buffers start their tasks later and waste safety margins.

Many organisations have developed a number of core approaches that have been adopted to battle these issues, such as Agile, Lean Product Development and, of course, Lean Manufacturing. Essentially, Lean thinking tackles the issue of human procrastination by making problems visible and encouraging people to tackle them with a high sense of urgency, and in a structured manner, but what it really does well is to focus on time, and the reduction of value stream lead-time in every aspect of an organisation, from customer interactions, to product development, manufacturing and supply chain.

These two elements of procrastination mean that we often avoid doing something until it's really necessary and also often take too long to 'perfect' something when there is time to spare. Whilst these two might

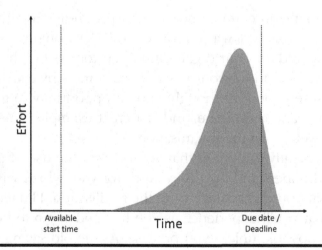

Figure 5.2   **Student syndrome**

seem mutually exclusive, or even contradictory, they actually feed into each other, as we spend too long working on the things that we like to do and fine tuning them right up to the deadline, whilst simultaneously avoiding the things that we don't like to do, or perhaps feel less competent in. When described in this way, do you recognise this in yourself? Perhaps this is something to consider as you practise your Hansei at the end of the chapter? Are you failing yourself through your natural bent towards doing what is comfortable and known to you, but perhaps not the most important of your priorities, whilst at the same time ignoring those things that really do matter, and leaving them incomplete or persistently late to deliver?

The Lean tools that I introduced for use on yourself will help you to tackle procrastination, but the potential irony is that you might procrastinate in starting to practise with them (Student syndrome) or you might spend too long on the ones that resonate with you the most (Parkinson's Law). As a strategy to tackle both these forms of procrastination, make a commitment to yourself to start practising with all of the tools, plan and manage your progress with your personal Kanban and utilise daily management to ensure that you follow through. Throughout the process, please use Hansei to reflect and learn as you progress, avoiding the trap of a PDCA approach, ensuring that you both feel and think about what is changing and inculcate it into your ways of working. As you experience the results of your changes, both emotionally and logically, you'll begin to believe in your new ways-of-working.

A little bit of knowledge is dangerous

The first bias barrier that I introduced to you in Chapter 2 was the Dunning–Kruger effect; what in layman's terms might be described as:

A little bit of knowledge is dangerous.

As you practise with the Lean tools, you must avoid declaring victory too soon and believing that you've become an expert, as I promise you that it's harder than you think to adopt and use them continuously and without losing focus during times of challenge or change. Entropy takes energy and persistence to resist, and is quick to set in when any form of disruption rears its head, and is just like a fitness regime or a diet in that it takes effort and discipline to stick to, but can be lost in a matter of hours. To combat this, it's important to focus yourself on following the competence development cycle, ensuring that you understand where you are on the cycle so that you can manage your own expectations of competence.

To get a human action to change permanently, the belief (wiring and firing pattern in the brain) has to change such that the new wiring (that is 'root cause' of new choices, actions and behaviours) is sufficiently strong enough to replace the wiring and firing patterns established over previous years of experience.

1. Unconscious incompetence: At its best this can be described as 'blissful ignorance' and in rare cases is a great enabler of innovation, as it allows people to attain results that normal paradigms may prevent them from achieving. However, generally this is not the case and 'not knowing what you don't know' is a real disabler of advancement. This is where the Dunning–Kruger effect can leave someone over-confident in their own ability due to a lack of knowledge of what they don't know.

2. Conscious incompetence: Once you realise what you don't know you can start to learn and this is an exciting time, particularly during times of change. In this phase you can read, experiment, study, hire external resources, team up with colleagues and other organisations to build solutions and fill knowledge gaps. This is where you'll be practising with the tools in a way that exposes more and more opportunity to develop yourself.

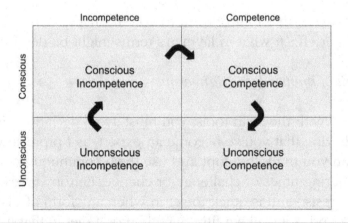

Figure 5.3   The conscious–competence learning matrix

3. Conscious competence: As you continue to develop your competence you'll become good at doing whatever you've been learning to do and will even start to create new insights and knowledge in this area. Here you start to become an expert in the subject and are conscious of this learning and of your knowledge.

4. Unconscious competence: At this stage you do things without even thinking and know things that you're not even conscious of knowing. This is what you observe when watching top sportspeople in action and when you work with people who are true experts in their field. This is true mastery but only when you are also able to shift back into conscious competence to teach and coach others when necessary. In fact that is one of the skills of a subject master, their ability to remember how they do things really well and the ability to explain it.

Whilst I was writing this chapter I coincidentally came across a post on LinkedIn by Tara Halliday,[2] in which she wrote about her mother doing what I think is a true example of a master willing and able to make herself consciously competent in order to better understand those less competent than her. This is the post (with the kind permission of Tara):

> *I found my mother reading a bridge book for beginners. This was odd as she's a Grandmaster bridge player and has represented her country in international bridge competitions.*
>
> *'Ah' I thought, 'she must be looking for a tiny gold nugget of bridge wisdom.'*
>
> *But as a serious player for the last thirty years, she's always had a bridge book on the go. That's a lot of books!*
>
> *Surely there was nothing she could learn from a beginners' book?*
>
> *When I asked her, she replied 'No. I wanted to remind myself of how beginners think.'*
>
> *It was a beautiful illustration of mastery.*
>
> *Growth is not just expanding into new territory. It's also deepening existing knowledge and experiences, and reviewing assumptions. And being open to new perspectives in ground you've already covered.*
>
> *It was a lovely lesson for me in high-performance skills and attitudes.*
>
> *Thanks, Mum!*

Tara Halliday • 1st
Neurodevelopment for Leaders | Inner Success training | Impostor Syndrome Sp...
9h • 🌐

I found my mother reading a bridge book for beginners.
This was odd as she's a Grandmaster bridge player and has represented the country in international bridge competitions.

'Ah' I thought, 'she must be looking for a tiny gold nugget of bridge wisdom.'

But as a serious player for the last thirty years, she's always had a bridge book on the go. That's a lot of books!

Surely there was nothing she could learn from a beginners' book?

When I asked her, she replied 'No. I wanted to remind myself of how beginners think.'

It was a beautiful illustration of mastery.

Growth is not just expanding into new territory.
It's also deepening existing knowledge and experiences, and reviewing assumptions. And being open to new perspectives in ground you've already covered.

It was a lovely lesson for me in high-performance skills and attitudes.

Thanks, Mum!

Figure 5.4 Tara Halliday's LinkedIn post

Once you understand the competence development cycle and can trace your own tracks through it, you can manage yourself as you practise and learn, helping to avoid the natural pitfall of the Dunning–Kruger bias and, as you gain mastery, being capable of taking others through their own learning cycle.

Hansei

Before moving onto the next chapter, please take a few moments to reflect and consider what, in relation to your own way of working and actions, are:

Your key learning points?

The changes that you could make?

Current problems that they would help to solve?

Notes

1 Critical Chain: A New Project Management: Paradigm or Old Wine in New
   Bottles? Thomas G. Lechler, Stevens Institute of Technology, Boaz Ronen,
   Tel Aviv University, Edward A. Stohr, Stevens Institute of Technology (2005).
   (http://boazronen.org/PDF/Critical%20Chain%20-%20A%20New%20Project%20
   Management%20Paradigm%20or%20Old%20Wine%20in%20New%20Bottles.pdf)
2 Bridge book for beginners post by Tara Halliday on LinkedIn (4th May 2020).
   (www.linkedin.com/posts/tara-halliday-phd_success-leadership-activity-
   6662956543660691456-Tr5V)

Chapter 6

Learning every day

It'll be alright in the end

There is a lovely saying in India:

> *Everything will be alright in the end. If it's not alright yet, then it's not the end.*

I really like the philosophy behind this as it supports the rationale that a positive outcome is a matter of time and effort, not a hit or miss, win or lose activity. With this thinking we can focus on learning every day and this will involve sometimes getting it right and sometimes it going in the wrong direction. Every day that we practise one or more of the nine Lean tools we are able to learn from the experience that it delivered. What had you hoped to realise from the use of the tool today and what did you actually achieve? Note the use of the term hope, as I'm focussing here on the BTFA cycle more than the PDCA cycle, and your emotional response to the success or failure of the outcome.

The idea that we can learn every day is much more of an emotional belief than a logical plan. Even though you and I could probably logically agree that we can learn something new every day, even if it's only something small, it really is the belief that we can do so that will help us to make the commitment to do so, and to invest that little bit of discretionary

DOI: 10.4324/9781003251385-8

effort that we need to exert to do so. This is because to learn something every day really is a choice to expend a little bit of your discretionary effort, effort that you wouldn't otherwise have to lay out, and that is something that requires you to truly believe in it emotionally and not just plan logically. You can't logically determine that you will become the best in your profession, field or sport, although you could make a logical plan to get there and use all of the information that you may glean to understand what it takes. That is valid and you do need to understand the path to be taken on your journey to achieve what you want. However, it is your faith in achieving your goals that will drive your commitment and keep you on the right path, the emotional conviction in your future that will drive your actions.

Failing is learning

The reason that you must have the emotional belief to make this philosophy work for you is that it'll involve failing every day. You might note that I have shamelessly used the word failure, which I do without apology because it's important that we don't hide reality behind a softening of our language. Failure is an integral part of learning, and when we're young we don't worry about it as we fall over when learning to walk, tumble from our bicycles as we take the stabilisers off them, or say 'maffise' when we mean 'massive', which is one of the many mispronounced words that I remember from my youngest daughter's development of her English language skills, and one which we still lovingly use for gentle fun occasionally.

Unfortunately, as we get older we become more self-conscious of failure and feel exposed through failure, sometimes to the point of creating a paralysis of action in taking the risks needed to problem solve and learn. Playing it safe becomes key to how we protect ourselves and we hide from the perceived negativity of failure, and the associated problems, by using language that hides from it. However, just as you've probably mastered walking, riding a bike and speaking your native language quite well (and I do apologise for my generalisation and assumption to anyone for whom a physical or mental challenge has made one of these things difficult or impossible), you can also master *Living Lean* if you are prepared to fail and learn from that failure.

Don't misunderstand me, I'm not suggesting that to adopt *Living Lean* you must take reckless risks. However, what I am proposing is that, when you've looked at the problems that you want to solve for yourself, perhaps something similar to the overwork example that I demonstrated earlier, an excessive meeting burden, or a feeling of being overwhelmed in meeting your deadlines, you can determine your goals and use the Lean tools to help you to solve them.

By doing so, I guarantee that you'll start to experience the improvements and begin to understand that this will be a transformation in your ways-of-working. However, you will sometimes fail, which is okay as you'll not experience abject failure, you'll instead experience some things working partially right and some things not right at all. It will be failure in the purest sense of the word but not something that is going to prevent you from getting better every day. Metaphorically speaking, you'll sometimes fall over and graze your knee, other times you'll take more steps than you've ever taken before. As Thomas Edison famously said:

> *I've not failed a thousand times, I've successfully found a thousand ways that do not work.*

This requires a conscious avoidance of blame, and the leader plays a big role in avoiding blame when others fail. The perception of failure is necessarily subjective through our own biases and filters, and leaders must therefore 'lead by example' if others are to avoid a fear-based reaction to change and failure. The key is in consciously creating the system and surroundings within which a major building block is the leader's attitude, words, emotional reactions, degrees of blame and projection, which in turn follow the leader's imprinted beliefs, self-conception and preconceptions of success. This unfortunately means that no individual can prevent the negativity of failure in isolation, as it's a socio-technical dance that the leader is central to. However, as is core to my personal beliefs and coaching of others, this does not prevent you, the reader, from taking up the challenge to practise failure in a positive manner and to take your own leadership and role-model approach to this.

Another important aspect of this mind-set is not to get caught in the 'talent trap', assuming that people who are really successful in their chosen field are born with the talent, or simply got lucky. Dr. Carol Dweck, in her million-copy bestseller *mindset*,[1] described how this type of thinking is what she calls a 'fixed mind-set' and explains this through examples of famous sports stars such as Mohammad Ali, Michael Johnson, Babe Ruth and Wilma Rudolph. These were arguably the most successful stars of their chosen sports, but she explains that they were not 'naturals' to their sports and that it was focus, hard work and discipline that were the real differentiators of their success.

Whilst I cannot do Dr. Dweck's book justice in a couple of paragraphs, in case you've just read the statement about those sports megastars and can't believe it, I'll summarise the example she gives of Michael Jordan, who was dropped by his high school varsity team, wasn't recruited by the college that he wanted to play for and wasn't drafted by the first two NBA teams that could have done so. In fact, when he was cut from his varsity team, his mother's response was that he needed to be more resolute in his discipline and practise more, which he did, and his dedication to practise continued to be legendary amongst the members of the NBA throughout his career.

As Dr. Dweck stated in her book, for Jordan success stemmed from the mind, whereas others only saw a physically perfected basketball player and assumed that his greatness was inevitable.

Learning a new golf swing

Anyone who's played golf for a serious amount of time will have reached a point in their performance whereby they need to change their swing to progress further. Unfortunately for most golfers, the difficulty of doing this means that many of them don't do so until they've hit rock bottom. If you think of this in the context of Lean and learning most people, and most organisations, tend to do the same, avoiding the required changes due to the difficulty of doing so, and really only doing it once they've hit 'rock bottom'. This is one of the reasons why we often hear metaphorical terms such as 'burning platform' when talking about the case for change and, even in those organisations that embrace a proactive case for change, it's almost inevitable that the leading parts of the business will be those that have significant issues of customer service, cash or profitability, whilst those parts of the business that are generally good are the laggards in their transformation. For most people and organisations, transforming from good to great is not often a motivating case for change.

I mentioned earlier in the book the issue of 'on top of' thinking about Lean and your need to avoid this. It's easier to put in place your leader standard work, to practise Kaizen and to do thorough problem solving when you're not under immense pressure. However, the times when you're under pressure, when you're forced into fire-fighting mode, are precisely the times when you need to be using Lean thinking to help you to solve the problems in the right way. However, I accept how difficult it is and it takes significant stamina to stay the course. Extending the golfing metaphor a little further, just as for the golfer when they start to swing the club differently, it feels uncomfortable to use Lean thinking rather than your well-established approach to problems. However, just as with the golf swing, it's not intended to be work in addition to what you already do but, rather, a fundamental change to your problem-solving approach.

Some people consider that the readiness for the adoption of Lean is once the organisation is stable, but this is the wrong way of thinking about things. How will you become stable by trying to tackle the problems causing the instability with the same methods that got you where you now are? My perception is that, when people talk about the need for stability before the implementation of Lean, they really mean that the organisation is unprepared for a fully-fledged Lean operating model, which is probably right. However, the wrong-thinking is that Lean is not the solution to the instability currently prevailing. Quite the contrary, it is needed more than ever and is analogous to someone who wishes to get fit; you wouldn't recommend or coach them in the same way as an Olympic athlete, but you also wouldn't tell them that it was okay to continue a sedentary lifestyle or an unhealthy diet. Rather, you would use 'health thinking' and be a fitness leader by helping them to adopt the right diet and fitness regime for them and this is precisely what you must do for yourself and your organisation; utilise Lean thinking to solve the stability issues that you face.

Consider Lean as a way of thinking and leading and apply the right tools and methodologies to resolve the issues that you, and your organisation, are facing. It will feel uncomfortable, and in some cases counter-intuitive, eliciting statements such as: 'We don't have time for this'. Nevertheless, the choice that you'll be making is whether to maintain the status quo and inevitable repetition of failure, or to make the change that will provide the stability that you desire.

Changing your proverbial golf swing will be uncomfortable, but it will be ultimately rewarding as your 'game' improves and you learn every day.

Winning is finishing

An important element of learning and being successful in what you do is to finish what you start. Dr. Travis Bradberry, LinkedIn influencer and co-author of Emotional Intelligence 2.0, wrote in one of his LinkedIn articles[2] about two really important elements of this thinking:

> *They finish what they start. Coming up with a great idea means absolutely nothing if you don't execute that idea. The most successful and happy people bring their ideas to fruition, deriving just as much satisfaction from working through the complications and daily grind as they do from coming up with the initial idea. They know that a vision remains a meaningless thought until it is acted upon. Only then does it begin to grow.*

> *They are resilient. To be successful and happy in the long term, you have to learn to make mistakes, look like an idiot, and try again, all without flinching. In a recent study at the College of William and Mary, researchers interviewed over 800 entrepreneurs and found that the most successful among them tended to have two critical things in common: they were terrible at imagining failure, and they tended not to care what other people thought of them. In other words, the most successful entrepreneurs put no time or energy into stressing about their failures as they see failure as a small and necessary step in the process of reaching their goals.*

There are two key points in what Dr. Travis says, firstly '...*that a vision remains a meaningless thought until it is acted upon*', and secondly '... *they see failure as a small and necessary step in the process of reaching their goals*'.

To win at what you want to achieve is not about luck, it's not about being naturally good at something, it's about setting stretching but attainable goals, planning them out well and then working hard to achieve them, with persistence, stamina and the willingness to face failure as an opportunity to problem solve and learn. Again, in the spirit of *Living Lean*, you win by facing up to small failures swiftly and with a positive perspective and as a result are able to avoid the large failures that are normally the result of ignoring the small problems. When you miss a deadline, it isn't often that it was a sudden failure that caused it. Instead, if you're honest with yourself, it was probably small failures to complete intermediate steps that resulted in the overall failure. If you didn't achieve the result that you wanted in your exam, it is likely that you missed some of the revision that you really ought to have done. That's human nature and the purpose of this book is not to criticise you or I for being human but to help us to manage our lives in a way that avoids large failures and helps to build our knowledge every day.

Consider Eliud Kipchoge and his record breaking marathon run.[3] On 12 October 2019 he ran a sub-two-hours marathon time of 01:59:40 in a special event in Vienna, which was meticulously planned with pacemaker runners and a special pacemaker car that projected green laser lines onto the ground to show Eliud the correct pace for him to achieve the sub-two-hours run.

If you relate this back to the concept of *Living Lean*, it demonstrates the need to develop a strategy and to deploy it through rigorous planning. This is what you see in the deep commitment by Kipchoge to the specific training that he had to undertake over many months. During the race he was effectively using 'daily management', following the pacing car that provided short-interval control, in effect unbroken and continuous visual control with a laser indicator that allowed him to follow the pace precisely to that scheduled as part of the planning. He could therefore 'problem solve' if he felt his pace faltering and ensure that any small problems of going slightly off-pace (either too slowly or too quickly) were responded to rapidly.

Whilst this is an extreme example of an elite within his profession, it serves as a clear example that simply having talent isn't what makes for success and that winning requires rigorous planning, and disciplined execution.

The acceptance of failure

We don't often want to speak about failure, especially in the context of business, as it elicits all sorts of negative emotions and there is the perception of blame towards and by anyone associated with it. Despite the many platitudes and assertions of learning through failing, and clichéd idioms such as 'fail fast, learn quickly' or 'innovation comes from failure', the vast majority of people will avoid like the plague the admittance of failure, or any association with it.

This is an important element of *Living Lean*, and is one of the key reasons why logical changes are often resisted, as the feelings evoked by a realisation that the current practices are not the best ways-of-working become feelings of failure, especially if the people involved have long tenure and might come to think that they might be blamed for not having already improved the processes. I'm sure that you can relate to this feeling; when someone observes or points out a better way of doing things that is logically better but emotionally hurtful. This is an important consideration for change and one that we all very often don't properly consider, getting caught up in the logical, project management approach to change.

Two important approaches to help to avoid the inevitable resistance of the feeling of failure is firstly to 'honour the past', ensuring that ample time is taken to understand the history of the organisation, function, department, site, or team, celebrate the past victories and successes, and use this as a motivator for future success. The second element, and central to *Living Lean*, is to ensure that the people who come up with the ideas, strategies and tactics for improvement are the people who do the work and will have to sustain the change. As Peter Senge[4] famously said:

*People don't resist change, they resist **being** changed*

This requires subtle and intelligent coaching, as many of the people involved will not understand how to make the changes or (yet) what changes to make. However, before getting to the point of the how and the what, *Living Lean* involves helping people to develop both their collective and personal whys. Why should they make the change? What's wrong with the current state? What's in it for them to change? Why should they put all of this additional effort in to make the change? Only once they **believe** that the change is necessary, can the approach, methodologies and tools required to understand the problem to solve (what can be improved), diagnose the reasons for the problem (root-cause analysis) and put in place the improvements (countermeasures), be taught.

This takes effort and, when there is a lot of pressure to get the results, from the customer, the leadership, shareholders, it can be extremely easy to simply take the PDCA route, which is logical, comfortable, easy to plan, and seductively easy to explain and comprehend. However, this approach will fail, as it will be an approach to change that does it to the people involved, instead of one that is about the people changing things for themselves. This doesn't mean that professional project management isn't required, as we certainly need to have proper control of resources, expenditure, deliverables, but the core message of this section is that the people involved must be an intrinsic part of the change, believing in the need, thinking through the process and outcomes, feeling part of the change and responsible for its success, and acting quickly to resolve problems. When this is achieved, the travails of change will not elicit feelings of failure; things will go wrong, failure will occur, but the emotional response to these failures will not be one of denial or concealment but instead problem solving and learning.

The maxim goes that:

Success has many fathers, failure is an orphan

Whilst the idiom is more accurately: Victory has a hundred fathers and defeat is an orphan, coined by Count Caleazzo Ciano (1903–44), and popularised by J.F. Kennedy after the Bay of Pigs fiasco, it's an important reminder of the natural bias for people to own success and disavow failure. *Living Lean* is therefore about how we ensure that our teams embrace their failures, rapidly solving the root causes and creating the success of which they may be proud.

However, there is a risk of contradiction in the notion of accepting failure: We must accept that we will fail sometimes, owning the failure and tackling it head on, but simultaneously be intolerant of failure, doing everything that we can, proactively tackling process issues to ensure that failure, particularly in terms of customer-facing failures, are prevented. There is an important differentiator that explains this dichotomy, that the acceptance of failure is unacceptable when it is related to repetitive failure; the tolerance of chronic problems that always occur, with the culture having developed around the mind-set of:

That's how it's always been

This acceptance is born from an externalisation of the root cause of the problem, a belief that this is out of the control of the people who do the work every day, and can exhibit itself as a 'victim mentality'. This might, in one sense, be true but, if you really aspire to be *Leading Lean by Living Lean*, we must ensure that we understand why this culture has developed and tackle those root causes. In Chapter 9 you'll read more about the culture cycle and how developing culture requires an intervention at the behavioural level, which is influenced both by the culture and the determinant of the mind-set that determines the culture. Only by understanding the reasons why the culture became one of tolerating failure can we intervene with activities that will change the behaviour and demonstrate the success that an intolerance of failure provides, through which we will change mind-sets and ultimately the prevailing culture.

As you've read the past few paragraphs, you will very likely have recognised that, once again, the discussion around the acceptance of failure has little to do with the logical (PDCA). The theme throughout this section has been about the emotional (BTFA), the beliefs that people have about their job, the processes that they work with, the environment that they operate within, and the leadership that they follow. The acceptance of failure is a double-headed coin, both an angel and a demon on the shoulder of us all, and the Lean leader must embrace their challenge to live and lead their colleagues along the right path.

Hansei

Before moving onto the next chapter, please take a few moments to reflect and consider what, in relation to your own way of working and actions, are:

Your key learning points?

The changes that you could make?

Current problems that they would help to solve?

Notes

1 *Mindset*, Dr. Carol S. Dweck. Publisher: Random House, ISBN: 978-1-4721-3995-5
2 Ten Things Successful People (Who Are Actually Happy) Do Differently, Dr. Travis Bradberry, LinkedIn influencer and co-author of Emotional Intelligence 2.0. (www.linkedin.com/pulse/things-successful-people-who-actually-happy-do-dr-travis-bradberry/)
3 Eliud Kipchoge is the IAAF (International Association of Athletics Federations) recognised Marathon World Record holder with a time of 2 hours, 1 minute and 39 seconds (02:01:39) set on 16th September 2018 at the Berlin Marathon. On 12th October 2019 he ran a sub-two-hours marathon distance of 01:59:40 in a special event in Vienna, Austria. Whilst not an official world record due to its non-adherence to pacing and fluid regulations, and also not being an open event, it is still recognised as the fastest-run marathon ever recorded. (https://en.wikipedia.org/wiki/Eliud_Kipchoge)
4 Peter Michael Senge (born 1947) is an American systems scientist who is a senior lecturer at the MIT Sloan School of Management, co-faculty at the New England Complex Systems Institute, and the founder of the Society for Organizational Learning. He is known as the author of the book *The Fifth Discipline: The Art and Practice of the Learning Organization* (1990, rev. 2006). (https://en.wikipedia.org/wiki/Peter_Senge)

Chapter 7

Kaizen every day

Running to standard

Whenever there is a problem, we should always first ask the question: *Are we running to standard?*

Many times the issue is simply that we've not followed the standard and we simply aren't doing what we ought to be doing. It can be hard to admit to ourselves that we've simply been human and not followed the standard but, if we are able to do so, we can avoid a lot of time wasted solving problems that don't, or at least shouldn't, exist. *Living Lean* is knowing that you don't need to reinvent everything and that using the standards that others have created is a fantastic way to then focus on applying your creativity to developing the next iteration of improvement.

Consider your favourite sport to participate in and how a game begins. It is highly unlikely that the players and officials would first discuss what the rules ought to be, other than some clarifications of some specific details, such as the toss of the coin. Can you imagine the disruption that there would be to an event, for example an international rugby game, if the coaches and players had to debate with the referee and their assistants on how long and wide the pitch should be, how many players would be allowed, what constitutes a ruck or a maul? It sounds ridiculous, doesn't it but, if you consider your daily life, how many times a day do you start meetings by discussing the 'rules of the game' rather than the real problems to be solved? It is therefore extremely important that you work with your

DOI: 10.4324/9781003251385-9

colleagues to ensure that you understand the 'rules of the game', the standards that have been set and documented in order that you don't have to have wasteful discussions and debates on a regular basis and, when new members of the team join, you can train them to these standards instead of leaving them to find their own way (and inevitably do it differently and in their own preferred way). This also applies to your personal ways-of-working, where taking the time to standardise what you do will help you to save time in the long term, as when you receive requests for reports, analyses, documents, etc., you will be well placed to do that efficiently and without expending excess time on them.

Once you've confirmed that you're working to the standard, it's then important to be realistic about the scale of improvements that you are able to make. In the long term everything is possible but often we can get stuck in a 'think big' mind-set, which can be debilitating as we focus on the big improvements, the step change initiatives, and wait for that great day when they solve all of our problems. 'When we have the new IT system in place everything will be okay', 'We just need the new CNC machine and then we can meet the quality specification and rate', are the types of statement that you might hear in the workplace. Unfortunately, the reality is that breakthrough improvement takes significant effort in terms of money, time and resource, and every organisation has limited resources to do so. Whilst it is true that breakthrough improvement is critical, we far too often neglect the small improvements as we await the 'holy grail' of tomorrow. This is where the mind-set that every little grain of improvement will contribute to a larger, cumulative impact on your performance is crucial. The improvement, what in Lean thinking we call Kaizen, doesn't need to be significant in itself; in fact that's the beauty of it, that it is quick and easy to implement, and when you implement Kaizen regularly you'll see your own performance, and subsequently that of your team and the organisation, improve.

That's not to say that we don't need step change improvement; quite the contrary, we need both step and continuous improvement, but focussing purely on projects and breakthrough improvements slows your own improvement and that of the organisation and means that each project has to resolve a number of ancillary issues in order to be successful (for example solving master data issues, or documenting process tasks) rather than building on solid foundations. Again, if you and your colleagues have solved the 'rules of the game' then breakthrough activity can be focussed on making the true step change that a new or improved technology will bring, rather than exhausting itself on fixing the fundamentals.

Kaizen is looking inwards

As discussed in Chapter 4, Kaizen are not simply good ideas but are rather the outcome of solving one of the three types of problem:

1. The standard is not achieved.
2. The standard is achieved but with high variation.
3. The current standard is achieved but a new standard is required.

Even in the early days of your transformation, when standards don't exist, you will essentially be solving problem type 3 whereby a new standard, the first-ever standard (version 1.0), is required. In Lean thinking organisations, every team member is challenged and empowered to constantly solve the three types of problem on a daily basis. Even when things are running well they will be given type 3 problems to solve, for example being asked to reduce the cycle time by 2–3%, and will normally solve it through the reduction of one or more of the 8 wastes.

I'm pretty certain that if you choose to reflect on this during your Hansei time at the end of the chapter you'll be struggling with a big gap between this philosophy and your own working practices; how many Kaizen did you personally implement in the last day, week or month? Was it a true Kaizen in that you solved a problem with the current standard (perhaps the problem was that there was no standard) and did you:

■ Run it through a 3C?
■ Identify one of the 8 wastes and tackle it with the countermeasure?
■ Implement a new documented standard?
■ Where the standard was not only related to your personal leader standard work, shared the new standard and had it agreed to as the new standard by all who use it?

The above seems like a lot of work, doesn't it? This is one of the reasons that I think that people find *Living Lean* such a challenge, as they are busy and therefore taking the additional time to invest in implementing Kaizen seems too much of a commitment for them. I'm sorry to say that I've not found an answer to easily convincing people to do so. Coaching, people reading my books, practising, and my personal role-modelling of the behaviour are the methodologies that I use, and many people have come on the journey with me as a result. Ultimately, though, it is only when you practise it for a prolonged period of time that you will experience and realise the overall time reduction that it provides for you, as well as the significant improvement in your performance that it delivers. This is because it will require the investment of time upfront and it can initially seem that you are doing all of the giving, contributing standards that benefit you but also your colleagues, who are not initially doing the same. Why should I do it if others aren't? That's a pretty human reaction, and completely understandable, which is one of the reasons why many people are resistant to practising Lean. However, part of being a Lean leader is to go first and to see the overall improvements and role-modelling of Lean thinking as a win–win, and take pride in the gifts of effectiveness that you are giving.

Over the years I would say that the most important thing that I've learned about Kaizen is the inward perspective that its practice promotes. Typically human nature is such that we look at others to improve our situation; we could do things really well if only others would change or if the systems were upgraded or fixed. However, we are much more the masters of our own destiny than we recognise, and we must therefore rid ourselves of excuses and prevarication, and instead focus on action and Kaizen. Most importantly we need to constantly remind ourselves that Kaizen is about looking inwards, not pointing blame outwards, which is a really challenging belief to foster as it demands that we take accountability for our personal contribution to problems and therefore their resolution, as opposed to the easier approach of blaming others. This is crucial in moving from a victim mind-set to one of a player mind-set: in the game, on the field and fighting to win, every day, through the improvement of your work.

When you first start to practise Kaizen you will likely find yourself offering others suggestions of how they should improve their working methods instead of looking at your own practices. That's human nature and we all do it, but it's so important that you begin to look inwards and consider what improvements you can make before advising others. The metaphor that I used earlier was to put your own oxygen mask on before helping others and that is critical here. As your working effectiveness improves others will see this and will want to emulate your success and that will be your opening to discuss where you might see improvement opportunities for them. As you put standards in place for you and your team's working practices you will begin to understand your processes better and be better able to see the myriad opportunities available to improve the elements of the processes that you own. Not insignificantly your colleagues, the downstream process team members and their customers (perhaps the end customer) will have observed the performance improvement and will be much happier in the relationship.

Looking inwardly is a core skill for *Living Lean*, as is the related practice of always beginning the problem solving with the question, 'What can I do to solve this?'

This will apply as much to your own personal standards as to that of the organisation's standards and, as is the theme in *Living Lean*, I really do encourage you to become a role-model in this regard. Show yourself and the organisation that the small amount of additional upfront effort to implement Kaizen every day will save a lot of time down the road as it avoids problems emanating from a lack of standardisation or from defective standards.

It doesn't need to be perfect to be better

Another barrier to Kaizen that I often observe is the human instinct to perfectionism, the instinctive need to fix all of the problems or the whole of a large problem. Whilst there are some problems that cannot be fixed piecemeal, these are in the minority and most of our problems are a network of ineffective or inefficient practices and, therefore, by making small changes every day, we can move our performance upwards in an incremental but ultimately significant way. You've probably heard or used the sayings 'Don't try to boil the ocean' and 'If you're eating an elephant, eat it bit-by-bit' and recognise the sentiments in these statements. However, it doesn't prevent us from falling into the trap of trying to solve problems completely or working on countermeasures ad nauseam. How often are you in meetings where someone (perhaps you) expands the conversation with a related but scope-expanding topic that makes the problem resolution more of a challenge than it already was? I would also expect that you've experienced a situation whereby a countermeasure was presented and someone raised a 'what-about?' item, which again might have been related but would increase the time to implement or would mean going back to the drawing board.

The crux of my point is that, both in our problem solving in teams and in our own individual issues, we must ensure that we focus on getting sensible incremental improvements in place through every day Kaizen, which will also help us to set in place more solid foundations for the solution of the larger problem overall.

Hoshin only works if you don't know how to do it yet

Whilst Kaizen every day is central to *Living Lean*, breakthrough thinking is also equally important, what in Japanese is called Kaikaku. At the end of the book I'll talk about how I used this approach to write this book in short-order and combined Kaizen to improve as I went.

Many readers will be familiar with the approach to deploying breakthrough initiatives in an organisation, called Hoshin Kanri (Policy Deployment or Strategy Deployment). However, whilst many organisations deploy this methodology, what many of them fail to realise is that:

> *If you know how to do it already, then it's not Hoshin Kanri!*

This results in the biggest barrier to effective Hoshin Kanri, which is changing the mind-set around setting the targets for Hoshin Kanri. Too often we get into 'horse trading', as the fear of failure limits people's willingness to sign up to targets that they don't yet know how to achieve. However, that's the spirit of Hoshin Kanri: 'shooting for the stars', and leadership behaviour plays a large part, whereby a target of 50% achieved to 37% needs to be seen as a success; to avoid setting targets of 10%, which are celebrated when 12% is achieved. Sandbagging has become an art form in many organisations.

> *Imagine if President Kennedy, instead of saying:*
> *'By the end of the decade we'll have put a man on the moon',*
> *had said:*
> *'By the end of the decade we'll have run tests to see the feasibility of putting a man on the moon, and we'll have sent up several space missions to establish the practicalities'.*
> *The scientists and NASA leadership might have felt more comfortable in their ability to achieve it but would have probably put a man on the moon much later (or been beaten to it by the USSR).*

Remember that many paradigms are only true until someone breaks them:

'It takes 5–10 years to develop an effective vaccine'.

'An electric car cannot have the same performance or attractiveness as a conventional internal combustion powered car'.

So the question that you need to ask yourself is: Which paradigms will you break?

Hansei

Before moving onto the next chapter, please take a few moments to reflect and consider what, in relation to your own way of working and actions, are:

Your key learning points?

The changes that you could make?

Current problems that they would help to solve?

HEART

Chapter 8

Feeling

We believe what we perceive

'Perception is reality' is a mantra I hear on quite a regular basis, which is a refrain used as a caution to us when we're struggling to understand why the facts that seem self-evident are viewed in a different light by others.

However, as Jim Taylor Ph.D. stated in a Psychology Today article,[1] 'perception is NOT reality'.

He then explained the dictionary differences:

Perception: *The way of regarding, understanding, or interpreting something; a mental impression.*

Reality: *The world or the state of things as they actually exist... existence that is absolute, self-sufficient, or objective, and not subject to human decisions or conventions.*

This means that the former is something that is an internal decision, based upon an individual's mental processing of their beliefs to create a view of the world, whereas the latter is external to the person and a fact. An example that Taylor gives is of a dog whistle being blown, which a human being cannot perceive (except where a dog is present and a secondary confirmation can be inferred), but that doesn't alter the fact that the dog whistle makes a sound.

DOI: 10.4324/9781003251385-11

This is why the *Feel* part of the Bovis cycle is so important, the experiential part of the cycle, and this will be crucial in your development of the skills in *Living Lean*, as the intellectual element will probably run ahead of the emotional experience. Your perception will be influenced by the bias barriers that I covered in Chapter 2 and therefore each reader will have a different experience as they go through the process. As I discussed in the previous chapter, to some extent you will probably experience the frustrations and questioning of the value of *Living Lean* in the early days, as you invest the time in properly problem solving and the creation of standards. As you go through this process you will be experiencing firstly the denial and then the frustration that the Kubler-Ross[2] model of change illustrates.

Some tips that Taylor gives for managing your perception during these processes:

- Don't assume that your perceptions are reality (just your reality).
- Be respectful of others' perceptions (they may be right).
- Don't hold your perceptions too tightly; they may be wrong (admitting it takes courage).
- Recognise the distortions within you that may warp your perceptions (seeing them will better ground your perceptions in reality rather than the other way around).
- Challenge your perceptions (do they hold up under the microscope of reality?).
- Seek out validation from experts and credible others (don't just ask your friends because they are likely to have the same perceptions as you).
- Be open to modifying your perceptions if the preponderance of evidence demands it (rigidity of mind is far worse than being wrong).

I had a big learning about this whilst working for Philips, at the time that I headed up procurement for the Mother and Child business, with the brand of Philips AVENT. We were faced with a growing concern in the marketplace about the issue of baby bottles made from polycarbonate, with the subject of concern being the residual monomer (the chemical that the plastic in question, polycarbonate, is made from) bisphenol A (BPA) and its risk of leaching into the baby's milk and subsequently being consumed. It had been experimentally shown in laboratory animals that BPA is an endocrine inhibitor, affecting the hormonal systems and potentially causing elevated rates of diabetes, some forms of cancer, reduced sperm counts, reproductive problems and other serious issues. However, all of the peer-reviewed scientific studies had shown that the amount of BPA residual in the polycarbonate, and the level that would or could leech into the milk, were far too low to be of concern. It was therefore decided by the business management team that this was not an issue that the business should be concerned about and that the continued manufacture of bottles in polycarbonate was the correct thing to do.

Nevertheless, as the weeks and months progressed it became clear that this was not the perception of the general public, particularly in the Californian market, where some research showed that mice drinking milk laced with BPA were experiencing serious hormone disruption issues, which, despite not being peer reviewed, was gaining serious traction in the minds of the public and legislature. However, the general view (or perception) of the management team continued to be that the science should come first in our decision making, which as an engineer I supported but as a parent I questioned. It was clear to me that parents would not take risks with their children and that if there was sufficient credibility in the message, they would respond accordingly. Their perception would trump ours, despite the relative scientific correctness.

The facts for us had to become the perception of our customers, not our perception of the science. I therefore became part of a small coalition who took a calculated business risk, with an associated personal career risk, to invest in new tooling, equipment and materials to produce baby bottles and soothers (dummies / pacifiers) from alternative BPA-free plastic materials. It was indeed a risk and if it had gone wrong my career might not have progressed in the way that it has, and I may not have written this book. However, the risk paid off and we secured the sustainment of €240M of business through a continuity of supply as BPA containing plastic baby bottles became unsaleable globally.

Change leadership

Throughout this process of personal change it is important to stay focussed on your VCRSP. Remember from Chapter 3 that, to be successful in your change to *Living Lean*, you must maintain all five elements to avoid failure.

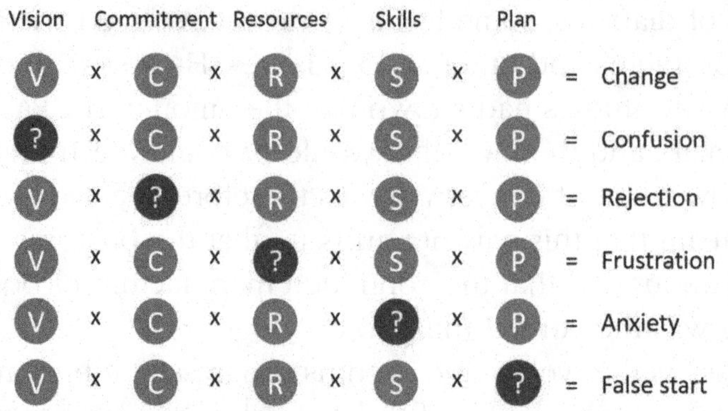

Vision		Commitment		Resources		Skills		Plan		
V	x	C	x	R	x	S	x	P	=	Change
?	x	C	x	R	x	S	x	P	=	Confusion
V	x	?	x	R	x	S	x	P	=	Rejection
V	x	C	x	?	x	S	x	P	=	Frustration
V	x	C	x	R	x	?	x	P	=	Anxiety
V	x	C	x	R	x	S	x	?	=	False start

Figure 8.1   The VCRSP model

I've repeated the graphic here to illustrate what you might have already noted, that the language used for each of the elemental failures includes emotional nouns:

■ Confusion
■ Rejection
■ Frustration
■ Anxiety

These are the types of feeling that you'll experience as you progress through any change process or transformation and your transition to *Living Lean* will not be any different.

Kotter[3] provided strategies for managing change in an organisation, which I covered extensively in *Leading with Lean*, and these can be pragmatically utilised in your own individual change process:

1. ***Create a sense of urgency:*** Set your vision around a clear reason for your desire to work differently, something that you truly believe in. No matter how good your vision, and how enthused you might be in the short term, the success of its attainment will hinge upon how much it really matters to you and therefore it must rest on a clear case for change, that creates a sense of urgency.

2. ***Build a guiding coalition:*** Gain as much support as you can for your change from people who can help you in its success. Can your manager help you in your change? Do you know of someone who can coach or mentor you, reaching out to them and asking for their support?

3. ***Form a strategic vision and initiatives:*** You will develop your vision, based upon a strong sense of urgency, and should use your personal Hoshin to develop the initiatives that you need to succeed.

4. ***Enlist a volunteer army:*** This is your personal development journey, but it doesn't mean that you must do it alone. You can enlist colleagues, family members and friends to support you and perhaps partner up with someone else who aims to start *Living Lean*.

5. ***Enable action by removing barriers:*** Identify the barriers to your success and work to remove them. Are you time poor? Then work on the time management tools to free up some time. Make some decisions to stop spending too much time on things that are not really a priority.

6. ***Generate short-term wins:*** Generating short-term wins is really important and as you practise the Lean tools you will start to have some successes that you will learn from but also, as we discussed in Chapter 6, you will experience some failures. The way that you deal with both will generate short-term experience wins that you can use to propagate your transformation.

7. ***Sustain acceleration:*** As discussed in Chapter 6, the stamina to continue to practise will be very important to your success and will ultimately be a result of having a persistent case for change and be built on support, success and learning.

8. ***Institutionalise the change:*** The best way that you can institutionalise change is through the Kaizen that you're going to focus on every day. Run to standard, problem solve and innovate with your creativity, implementing Kaizen as you go. Following the standards that you've set with your new methodologies will mean that your meetings are more effective, your time is managed much better and you continuously improve.

The language of avoidance

The language that we choose to use is important in the way that we process the information that we receive from it. As I've discussed in earlier chapters, our perception of reality is influenced by the words that we choose and the emotions that we attach to them. Tardiness, the habit of lateness, is a really good example of this, as being late is in many cases a decision that we make on a regular basis, although the language that we use doesn't usually establish the admission of the choice that we made.

We are late for meetings, appointments, responding to emails, delivering to project deadlines, dropping our kids off at school, completing applications, revising, and numerous other things, and in many cases the consequences are relatively minor. However, in some cases the consequences can be much more serious, such as the accidents caused by rushing, speeding, distraction or carelessness resulting from lateness. In an organisational context, tardiness causes all forms of disruption, as well as disharmony in teams due to the impact that it has on trust and effectiveness.

Dr. Neel Burton wrote an article in Psychology Today about the psychology of lateness,[4] in which he highlighted some of the reasons for lateness, such as a lack of self-knowledge, empathy or willpower. Burton states in his article that being late could be perceived as a message that says: 'My time is more important than yours'. Nevertheless, what I'd like to focus on is the language that we use and its impact on mind-set and the cognitive dissonance that it can cause. Here are some examples:

What you say: Sorry that I'm late, I was tied up in the earlier meeting.
The reality: I chose to stay in the previous meeting, considering it a higher priority to this meeting.
What you say: Sorry that I'm late, it is a 10-minute walk between buildings.
The reality: I decided to leave insufficient time to get to your meeting.

Whilst the reality that I've described might seem a little harsh (emotionally, rather than logically speaking), it's the importance of the acceptance of the *decisions* that we have made when we're late that will allow us to improve and to avoid chronic lateness. For example, did the traffic really make us late, was it unpredictable or an anomalous day for traffic, or was it totally predictable and we simply didn't set off in time? Did we really get held up in the previous meeting or did we make a decision to allow it to overrun, or did we leave insufficient time to move between locations? Ultimately there may be many pressures that we feel under to make decisions that make us late: the demands of family life, the seniority of the person running the previous meeting, social convention making it easier to be late than to say that you can't make it at that time, a lack of trust in the team or organisation that inhibits our willingness to be honest about what we're able to commit to, and many others. I've spent a great deal of Hansei time considering it and believe that, ultimately, the only way that we can improve is to be honest with ourselves about what drives our decisions and what we can and want to do about it. Will changing the language of lateness help us in our personal and professional lives? I think so, and would encourage you to consider what it might mean for you.

It is not just time keeping that engenders the language of avoidance, as there are also many examples of this in meeting projects or other commitments. For example, if you are on a fitness training programme and have made a great start to it, it can be very easy to come up with excuses as to why it's acceptable not to go for your planned run that day:

> *'I'm already ahead of target'*
>
> *'I'm tired'*
>
> *'It's too cold, it could be dangerous to run in this weather'*
>
> *...and around another dozen or so excuses, which I'm sure that you can all think of (and have used).*

If we consider our time both at work and in our personal lives, it's far too easy to make excuses for doing less than we've promised ourselves, finding reasons why it's okay not to meet targets, follow standards, deliver to deadlines, meet the commitment, turn up to the meeting, or numerous other things that we ought to do but somehow manage not to. This language of avoidance is embedded in our human nature and I don't intend to criticise anyone for it; we're all human and our flaws are sometimes our most endearing features. However, if we're able to minimise the urge to make excuses, and instead focus on delivering to our commitments, we will succeed in attaining our long-term goals. One of the issues with excuses is that they are rewarded in a short timescale, whereas following through on commitments (either to yourself or others) takes a lot longer to provide a payback.

In the earlier example of not going for a run, the short-term 'reward' of staying in the warm, resting and reading, listening to some music, or watching a little TV would give you an almost immediate payback. However, the decision to go for a run would mean that you have to endure the cold and a hard slog of a run before getting the payback of the feeling of pride for having made the run. The health benefits of the run are also very difficult to observe on a single occurrence. This is similar in the workplace, where not following the standard work, taking that short cut to get the job done 'quicker', not meeting the deadline, etc. provide some short-term relief to someone who is very busy, possibly feeling overloaded, and perhaps worried about looking bad if they admit that they have a problem. Many traditionally managed organisations promote the 'need' of their people to embrace the ease of excuses, leaving individuals to manage their own work in the best way that they know how, providing little or no direction and without adequate prioritisation. In fact, getting 'quick' solutions to problems is actively rewarded and, in a busy environment, will be appreciated by many of the leaders as it will get it off their desk in the short term.

Living Lean promotes an honesty in our language, at least to ourselves, so that we can develop our ability to meet commitments through a focus on them and the actions that we must take to meet them. If we've overcommitted, instead of making excuses for it we will accept the over-commitment, problem solve, and course-correct to determine more realistic targets.

Excuses are easy and provide short-term relief, but having the discipline to plan, manage and deliver upon commitments is far more rewarding in the long term.

Hansei

Before moving onto the next chapter, please take a few moments to reflect and consider what, in relation to your own way of working and actions, are:

Your key learning points?

The changes that you could make?

Current problems that they would help to solve?

Notes

1 Perception Is Not Reality, Jim Taylor Ph.D., *Psychology Today*, 5th August 2019. (www.psychologytoday.com/gb/blog/the-power-prime/201908/perception-is-not-reality)
2 The Kubler-Ross model of change was developed based initially on the stages of grief but later developed to demonstrate the emotional phases that people experience whilst going through most types of change.
3 John Kotter is a *New York Times* bestselling author and is considered by many as the authority on change leadership. He promotes his thought leadership through his company Kotter International and is an international speaker and Harvard professor.
4 The Psychology of Lateness, Neel Burton M.D., *Psychology Today*, 16th June 2014. (www.psychologytoday.com/gb/blog/hide-and-seek/201406/the-psychology-lateness)

Chapter 9

Winning hearts

Developing the change

As is the theme of this book, metaphorically putting on your own oxygen mask before that of others provides you with a much higher degree of credibility in what you advocate, and will give your colleagues the confidence that you are not only asking them to be part of the Lean transformation but are truly living it. *Living Lean* is authentic; it's a real difference in the way that you work and when you live it you can help yourself and others to benefit from a transformed way of thinking and doing. For those of us who've been through the journey over a number of years, and have worked within an organisation that had adopted Lean thinking to the point that it had become a part of the culture, the difference is phenomenal.

However, well before we get to this change being truly part of our culture, we have to begin the change, and that starts with an intervention at the behavioural level. The culture cycle, as I described in *Leading with Lean*, is a reinforcing cycle:

1. Behaviours are reinforced by either positive or negative feedback.
2. The consistent repetition of behaviours, over an extended period of time, creates a mind-set, a belief in what is true.

DOI: 10.4324/9781003251385-12

3. As the mind-set pervades a group of people, it becomes part of the culture of the organisation.
4. The culture reinforces the behaviours of the people within the organisation.

Intervention at the behavioural level is therefore the approach which will create the change that we aspire for. Please note, though, that this cycle works for both positive and negative behaviours, and both describes the process by which a culture is created and reinforces the behaviours and mind-set that prevail within an organisation. It is therefore crucial that the Lean leader promotes the right behaviours by living Lean and role-modelling.

I've used the term journey a lot in the book, and it has become something of a cliché, especially within business. However, when I considered the right descriptor to use, it became clear that journey was the correct word, especially when you consider the synonyms:

Expedition, trek, hike, march, trudge, voyage

If you think about their meanings, it is clear that they describe many of the challenges that I've described in *Living Lean*, and it could be no more pertinent than when it comes to winning the hearts of our friends, colleagues and family members. As you practise the tools described in the book, you'll be developing your change through the internalisation of the experience. Your changed behaviours will be experienced as you

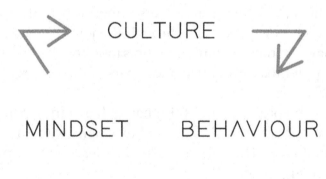

Figure 9.1 The Culture Cycle

run through your PDCA–BTFA cycles of learning, and with the positive reinforcement that you will feel, your mind-set will transition and you will begin to believe. With this new belief you will become a role-model and evangelist for *Living Lean*, espousing the advantages that you've derived and showing your friends, colleagues and family how they can also benefit from the investment in a new way of being.

Keeping it simple

One of the best ways to win hearts is to make some quick wins and to do so with some simple but meaningful changes. A great example of this was Mary Barra, CEO of General Motors, who in 2009 made what she called the 'smallest biggest change' she had made.[1] Barra became VP for Global HR and discovered that the HR team were working on an extensive dress code, with regulations such as: 'You can't wear T-shirts that have words on them that could be misinterpreted'. The policy was 10 pages long and so, after some consideration, she instead replaced it with the statement:

> *Dress appropriately*

She had some pushback from managers, such as a senior manager who said that he had been embarrassed by team members wearing jeans to important meetings, but she countered by asking him whether he'd actually had a conversation with his team about it, to which he answered that he hadn't. Two weeks later he reported back that a conversation with his team had resulted in them wearing jeans for their regular working time, but keeping dress pants in their office drawer in case they were needed for a meeting. The ethos behind this approach by Barra was that managers must lead; they must take ownership for their team members and be accountable for leading them. What could this mean for you? How could you address some of the complexities in your life, either personal or professional, to simplify things to a two-word statement of intent? Do you have long policies or complicated procedures that no-one reads or that you have long discussions about to define and redefine what they actually mean? If this is the case then you'll probably find that it's the shared values and vision that are missing, rather than more words in a document. Consider, perhaps during your end of chapter Hansei, how you could work with your family, friends and colleagues to think differently about your norms and to establish a values rather than rules-based way of approaching the everyday behavioural decisions to be made, like the 'how to dress?' question.

Remember that we are striving for excellence and, as a statement often attributed to Aristotle opines, that:

We are what we repeatedly do. Excellence is not an act, but a habit.[2]

The risk is that we attempt to attain excellence to such an extent that we over-complicate it, something that I've often struggled with. It's a real dilemma, because excellence cannot be achieved if everyone simply does their own thing, as that is where chaos lives and is why unstable and dysfunctional organisations are often so frustratingly hard to rescue, as the individuals in them are all working to do the best that they can, but often unintentionally working contrary to their colleagues' best intentions. At the same time, if we over-codify every aspect of how to operate, it will drive disengagement and disinterest, as we can get to the point that we need a Philadelphia Lawyer to explain the minutia of detail in the standards.

We therefore require a sensible balance of general intent and explanation of the standards that really matter, such as a clear balance can be made. This is the sometimes unicorn-like goal for the Lean leader, who will spend a significant amount of their time trying to attain this balance, knowing that to win hearts and minds the standards, and overarching operating model, must be something that people can readily engage with.

Balancing simplicity with the need to set clear standards is further complicated by those who will resist the change and conspire to find reasons why it will never work. The standards that are set will always be a problem for them and it is imperative that you don't compromise your goal of *Living Lean* by constantly trying to adapt to their ongoing and changing criticisms of the system. This is what was introduced to me as not responding to 'the negative two', which refers to the two–six–two rule of change, whereby for every 10 people in the organisation, there will be two people who are avid supporters, or promoters, of the change, six people who are ambivalent, or waiting to see whether it begins to make a positive difference, and then two people who are avidly against the change, or act as detractors. A substantial amount of time can be spent trying to appease the negative two, which will lessen you from spending time engaging with the promoters and in bringing along the undecided. *Living Lean*, of course, begins with yourself and you will therefore learn what is working and what isn't through your own practice of being a Lean leader, which helps you to both understand and to role model Lean leadership.

Living Lean can be an inspiration for all if it shows that life can be easier and the bureaucracy reduced. This will also help to fight the misapprehension that standards create bureaucracy and reduce creativity, and instead demonstrate the multitude of benefits that they can bring.

Communicate to inspire

One of the key reasons why winning hearts is so challenging is that most of us think in the opposite direction of what's needed to be successful. As Simon Sinek explained very well in his seminal book *Start with Why*,[3] most people think of, and explain, things in a way that starts with describing what it is that they're going to do and achieve, before then covering how they're going to do it before, if in fact they even get to this point, why it's required. Sinek describes how those people who create movements think and talk in the opposite way, starting by creating a picture of the why and winning over people to their cause, before next describing the how and engaging their followers in its creation. Finally, and only then, they get to the what, which almost takes care of itself. He uses examples such as Martin Luther King Jr. and the Wright Brothers to illustrate that they were not the best placed to be the leaders of their respective movements, with fewer resources and influence at the start, but that their way of thinking attracted more followers and successes in the long run.

If you consider what we've discussed throughout *Living Lean*, it might have become clear that this *Start with Why* approach is embedded within its philosophy. Despite the sections being in the order of Head, Hands and Heart, I hope that you can see the why in each of the sections, and the focus on developing the why in everything that we do. Inspiration, large or small, is required for us all to make a change; we must believe that what we are going to do really matters and is important to us. Your journey to think and behave differently every day is no exception, and it is important that the language that you use to determine and reinforce what you are going to do inspires you, and those who you collaborate with, to endure and maintain your stamina throughout the transformation.

David Bovis[4] opined on the subject of language:

> *Our brain uses language in more ways than you can imagine, which has led to me claiming (more than once) that: 'Culture pivots on language'.*

Language literally stimulates the growth of neurons, forming our brain and our beliefs. The BTFA model shows us that our beliefs sit at the root of our behaviours, attitudes and actions. Therefore, if we want to change performance, it's imperative to change the language register that we employ on a daily basis. Talking of project management, KPIs, Lean tools and EBITDA isn't enough; we must also talk about brains and minds wherever people form part of our socio-technical landscape.

That's what makes the BTFA model so powerful: It's your entry point to a new world view about what 'good' looks like. Without new language, you can't ask new questions, and without new questions, you will only get old answers.

If you want culture change, step one is BTFA. Only then can you really make the transformation that you want and need.

Hansei

Before moving onto the next chapter, please take a few moments to reflect and consider what, in relation to your own way of working and actions, are:

Your key learning points?

The changes that you could make?

Current problems that they would help to solve?

Notes

1 GM CEO Mary Barra Explains How Shrinking the Dress Code to 2 Words Reflects Her Mission for the Company, Business Insider, 27th March 2015. (www.businessinsider.com/gm-ceo-mary-barra-on-changing-gms-dress-code-2015-3?r=US&IR=T)

2 The quotation: 'We are what we repeatedly do. Excellence is not an act, but a habit', is often attributed to Aristotle but it is unlikely that he wrote it. It is much more likely that it was coined by Will Durant in *The Story of Philosophy: The Lives and Opinions of the World's Greatest Philosophers*, published in 1926. The quotation was certainly inspired by the musings of Aristotle but unlikely to have been something written that translated as succinctly or poetically into English.

3 *Start with Why*, Simon Sinek, Publisher: Portfolio (2011), ISBN13: 9781591846444

4 David Bovis, founder of Duxinaroe (www.duxinaroe.com/) and creator of 'The Psychology of Change'.

Chapter 10

Living Lean

Urgent – important conflict

One of your biggest challenges to *Living Lean* will be the daily test of deciding what you should be spending your time on. The way of thinking and the tools that I've described are all designed to support you in ensuring that you spend your time on the important elements of your life and not the insignificant things that waste your time and detract from its meaning. For many people the driver of their activity is whatever the latest request is to them, particularly if it's from their boss. Therefore they are significantly driven by email coming at them, an ad hoc call or the latest meeting that they attended. They start the day with a plan, the first 'shot of battle' is fired, and their day ends after a whirlwind of activity but with little of their original plan completed.

Does that sound like many of your days? If so there's a danger that you've become trapped in the urgent–important trap and that this conflict is having a deleterious impact on your daily professional and personal life. As I'll discuss in the next section, to some this is actually a reassuring feeling, as in the short term it's simpler and easier than the alternative of running a planned and organised day, focussed on delivering what really matters.

DOI: 10.4324/9781003251385-13

Figure 10.1   The Urgency–Importance matrix

The Urgency–Importance matrix is well known and used extensively by many, although I've amended it slightly from the normal illustration in two ways:

1. Instead of **Do** and **Plan** for the important activities, I've called them **Focus** and **Schedule**.
2. Instead of **Delegate** for the low-importance, high-urgency activities, I've called it **Challenge**.

The reason for the first change is that, with the learning that I've provided in this book, I believe that you can live a life whereby you reduce the important–urgent items to only those that you are focussing on in your personal Kanban, and have those important items not yet urgent scheduled and ready for on-time delivery. This means that you know what you need to do, have it planned and scheduled as part of your leader standard work, and deliver consistently what is needed at the required level of quality and on time. Certainly there will be special cases and unanticipated issues will raise their head but, as we have discussed throughout the book, this is why you want to be organised to deliver those things that you already know how to do: so that you're in a state of readiness for the unexpected. Just as a top professional athlete has practised the standard routines of their sport to the point that they don't need to think about them and are able to respond quickly to their opponent's attack, so you can be ready for the unexpected and rise to the challenge.

The intent of the second change is that the instruction to delegate the low-importance, high-urgency items can be dangerous and misleading. If it is really a case that these activities or tasks must be done and the level of importance is relative to whether it requires your attention or someone else's (for example a more appropriately skilled colleague, a member of your team or another family member), then I would agree that delegate is a valid approach. However, often it is the case that the activity is actually not important at all and ought not to be done and so a delegation simply gets it off your plate and onto someone else's, which is not what we want to achieve. Instead let's challenge the validity of those tasks that we believe sit in the urgent–unimportant quadrant and determine whether they are necessary at all or are simply wasteful activity that should be discontinued or eradicated. Try to understand from where the urgency is manifesting itself. Is it someone senior for whom it's a 'pet project' or is there a misconception in the organisation about it and the perception of others is that it's actually important? Are you wrong about it being unimportant and it actually is important and you need to reposition it in the matrix and act accordingly? Whatever the outcome, hopefully it's clear why I think that challenge is a much better approach than to simply delegate.

In summary, the four quadrants should be dealt with in the following manner:

> ***High importance – High urgency:*** Focus on these items, ensuring that they are the activities that you are working on as part of your current personal Kanban.
>
> ***High importance – Low urgency:*** Schedule these items in your personal Kanban to ensure that you do them on time and to the right quality level, with adequate preparation and to standard.
>
> ***Low importance – Low urgency:*** Eliminate anything in this quadrant as it shouldn't be worked on at all.
>
> ***Low importance – High urgency:*** Challenge the need for these activities and understand from where the urgency is manifesting itself. Determine whether it is in the correct quadrant, eradicate if possible and, if necessary, delegate it if you are not the best person to undertake it.

Lean busy or ignorant overloaded bliss

Being too busy, overloaded, is something that *Living Lean* aims to avoid but that shouldn't be confused with not being busy. You will be busy executing what matters with a high degree of effectiveness but taking adequate breaks and completing your work in time to also spend personal time on what matters to you. However, for people in the early stages of their transition, the perception can be different. A good example of this is that for many people on their Lean journey a great way of seeing what world class looks like is attending best-practice visits to operationally excellent companies on bench-marking, or Kaikaku, experiences. However, one consistent feedback that I receive from participants, especially those to Toyota, is that they are impressed but:

> *'I wouldn't want to work there.'*

When this is probed further, the underlying reason is that they observe team members who appear to be constantly busy and that the work must be tiring and monotonous, working to the cadence of their standard work, whether operator, support staff or managerial, all aligned to the Takt time of the customer demand. This is always intriguing to me as, over the many years of practising Lean leadership and studying many world-class organisations, I have come to the conclusion that the real issue is that Lean organisations 'make problems visible', the problem in this case being that to be a world-class organisation it takes focussed, deliberate and consistent effort to meet a customer's sustainability, innovation, quality, cost and delivery requirements. In these operationally excellent organisations the magnitude of the task, and the way that it is solved, are blatantly obvious to all, and their people are trained and engaged in being up to the task. Just like a top-performing sports team, they know that it takes training, hard work, persistence and innovation (Kaizen) to succeed, and they all understand their 'field position' in the team's success.

Contrast that with a traditionally managed organisation, where processes are loose and ambiguous, standards weakly applied and competence development poor. In those organisations the solution to the problem of meeting their customers' needs is not so obvious, and people have much more perceived autonomy to do the job at their own pace. However, the irony is that when I discuss the biggest issues that people have in traditional organisations, it is their overload: long hours, stress, too many meetings to attend, continually having to deal with recurring problems. The very symptoms that they perceive to exist in Lean organisations are the very symptoms that they acutely suffer from in their own organisation. There is certainly a perception versus reality conflict in terms of how people are unable to see the freedom that these Lean organisations create for the people who work there.

For many the reality of being 'Lean busy' is undesirable compared to the ignorant bliss of the overload in their traditional organisations and in my experience this is a significant barrier for many organisations in their Lean transformations. However, before that it begins with the individuals, with you the readers and your own battle with the recognition of the many benefits that a change in your way of working, to a more structured and coordinated approach, will provide you with the time to spend on the things that really matter to you.

Living Lean

As you practise *Living Lean* you're going to be on a rollercoaster ride of highs and lows. Will you have the stamina to see it through or will it become too much of a change to be able to keep it going and you'll find that you revert to your 'normal' behaviours? It isn't easy and as you go through this you'll probably observe, as I often do, that even those people with Lean, Continuous Improvement, Six Sigma or Operational Excellence in their job title don't often actually operate in the way that they teach and coach others to do. In fact, I've met a number of Lean consultants whose working practices could benefit from *Living Lean*!

For those of you who stay on the track, your colleagues, friends and family will ask you how you managed to complete that report so quickly or solve that problem so rapidly. 'How do you manage to get so much work done; you must be working long hours?' will be a question that you hear regularly, although that won't be the case because, as I discussed earlier, you will have increased the amount of your time that adds value instead of increasing the hours that you work. I've been practising Lean for longer than I've been living it, and I can honestly tell you that I only really got to the point that I could consider myself an expert worthy of advising others when I truly started to 'practise what I preach' and 'Walk the Talk'. We've all heard the story of the doctor who drinks too much Scotch whiskey or the police officer who drinks and drives, but do we really want to be coached by a Lean expert who works in a traditional manner? However, once again the point of this book isn't to look outwardly but inwardly, and what I hope that it has helped you to determine is how *Living Lean* can help you to meet your personal improvement goals and to live both your personal and professional life in the way that you want to do. To achieve this you'll need to have the knowledge, skills and desire to do it and I can, through this and my other books, help you with the knowledge; following the advice and practising will help you with the development of the skills but, ultimately, it will rest on you having the continued desire to make the change.

We talk a lot about a life in balance but perhaps we should, instead, think about the rhythm of our lives; instead of balancing the content of our life, we should ensure that we create a daily, weekly, monthly rhythm that works within our physical, mental and financial limits. If we're not careful, we can easily continue to balance our life scales until there's a massive load on each side, ultimately breaking and collapsing under the total weight. However, if we think about creating rhythm, we should be able to quickly identify when we're 'out-of-tune' and do something about it. Perhaps think about that in your Hansei and consider how thinking differently about your life's 'Takt' could liberate the way that you deal with it.

I sincerely hope that *Leading Lean by Living Lean* has helped you to decide upon the next step in your personal development and I would encourage you to use the five-point change self-assessment that I introduced to you in Chapter 2 on an ongoing basis.

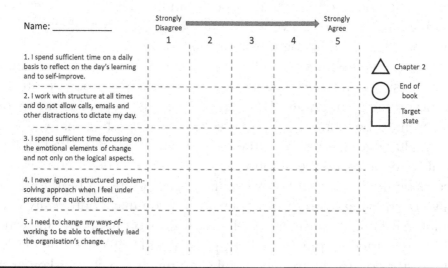

Figure 10.2   5-point change self-assessment

Thank you for buying my book and for taking the time to read it but, before I finish this chapter and the summary of the 'Heart' section of the book, I want to ensure that I haven't given you the wrong message. *Living Lean* isn't a 'one size fits all' approach to your personal and professional life and the way that I do it is most likely not going to work for you. The fact that you've bought a book with this title probably means that you don't mind the term Lean but, if you prefer to avoid the term, do so. If you don't like the Japanese terms such as Kanban, Hoshin, Kaikaku, etc., then ditch them but please consider whether you're doing so for the right reasons.

As with my other two books, I've written *Leading Lean by Living Lean* to share my knowledge and experience with others, in the sincere belief that this will help them to work and live better and make their, and by extension our, world a little bit better. I therefore really hope that you've gained the knowledge and inspiration that will help you to achieve this end and I'd really like to know how it has impacted you, which you can most easily do via LinkedIn or via my website, leadingwithlean.com. I started the book by explaining that it's not intended to be a self-help book but rather a self-reflection book, and that it will provide you with information to help you make a change, but change will only be made if you choose to do so. Whilst everyone who reads this book will read the same words, sentences, paragraphs and chapters, each reader will have a unique experience of the book and take from it different things, hopefully those things that make a positive difference for them.

Whatever you've taken from it, I'm firstly pleased that you've made it to the end section and secondly hope that what you've taken from it will help you not to change who you are but to change what you do!

Hansei

Before moving onto the next chapter, please take a few moments to reflect and consider what, in relation to your own way of working and actions, are:

Your key learning points?

The changes that you could make?

Current problems that they would help to solve?

WALKING THE TALK IV

Chapter 11

Writing the book

Writing Lean

Like you I have a demanding job, which along with my personal life
consumes a lot of my time. Fortunately through *Living Lean* I've been
able to allocate time to write three books over the past five years. At the
beginning of the year 2020 I planned to write the manuscript of this book
as part of my personal Hoshin, and had it scheduled as a six-months
endeavour for the second half of the year. However, when the COVID-19
crisis hit and we went into lockdown, I saw an opportunity to spend
some of the time that I would be in the house to accelerate the writing of
the book but, probably more importantly from an emotional perspective,
provide myself with an additional sense of control, purpose and self-
development. I therefore targeted the manuscript completion over a 12-
week period, beginning on the weekend of the 10th April 2020. I felt that
this was achievable as, in contrast to my previous two books, I intended
this to be a shorter, self-development book, which would be in the range
of 30–40,000 words, allowing the reader to gain some practical inspiration
to begin their life-changing journey but without it being an overload of
information.

I therefore determined the best timeslots for writing the book at the
weekend, with an overflow into the weekday evenings, taking into account
my other personal commitments and planning it out in my personal
Kanban. I then adopted a simple, visual daily management approach to

DOI: 10.4324/9781003251385-15

track my word count delivery performance over the period of time (short-interval control, visual management) and a self-assessed quality rating for what I'd written in that weekend. I used the Pomodoro technique to ensure that I managed my time and energy levels and provided myself with adequate rest periods. I then got to work writing the book, taking the initial concept that I held in my mind into a skeleton outline, a rough table of contents, and in the first weekend made fantastic progress. I'd set myself a vision, I was committed, I had the resources to do it, my previous two books had honed my writing skills, and I had a plan – VCRSP was all green and so I began.

What I think was interesting was that I actually completed the manuscript in seven weeks, exceeding my word count every week and with a high level of motivation, which I don't believe would have been attained without the Lean thinking approach that I took to achieve it. The qualitative approach to the quality of my writing also really helped, as it was a good counterbalance to simply getting words on the page and, in the graphic, you can see that I had a week where I rated my quality very low. The quality rating was based upon a self-assessed scale of 1 (low) to 5 (high), which I needed to mark myself on dependent upon my reading of what I'd done that weekend, and in the first three weeks I rated myself as 4, 4 and 5, respectively, against a target level of 4. However, in week four I read my content and didn't feel that it was good enough, which also prompted me to look at the overall book's flow and cohesiveness, which prompted me to rate a level 2 and undertake some problem solving.

The result of the problem solving was a rewrite of some of the earlier elements and a slowdown in my words per weekend, still over the target but with a more considered writing approach and a resultant increase in my quality assessment, which I maintained over subsequent weeks. Ultimately only you, the reader, can say whether the quality meets your expectations

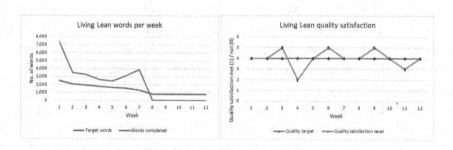

Figure 11.1   *Living Lean* short interval control

but after the completion of my manuscript I also had trusted members of my network, and my publisher, read and provide feedback, which helped tremendously in the finalisation of the book. However, I hope that you can see how the fact that I am *Living Lean* was a tremendous help in achieving the best possible book with an optimal mix of quality, cost (time expended) and delivery (lead-time to write).

The last element of writing the book was a decision I made to trial writing in threes, as I'm a big fan of the power of three in communications and the principle of the Head, Hands and Heart was already built around this premise. The power of three in communications can be traced back to ancient Greece and was emulated by Thomas Jefferson in the U.S. Declaration of Independence and the pursuit of life, liberty and happiness.[1] Its basis may be found all around us and so it seemed like an interesting experiment to write *Living Lean* in this manner. I therefore split the book into three chapters for each of the three elements of head, hands and heart and then each chapter into three sections. This allowed me to ensure that each element was evenly covered and that each chapter had a good balance. Hopefully you also found it useful in it being easier to read, more easily understood, better content, and more relevant for you.

What I left out

As I mentioned in the previous section I wanted *Leading Lean by Living Lean* to be shorter and easier to read than my previous two books, as the focus was different. In *Leading with Lean* I wanted to equip someone to tackle the immense challenge of transforming their organisation through a Lean transformation using Lean thinking, and in *The Simplicity of Lean* I wanted to support the Lean practitioner in applying Lean thinking in a meaningful and effective way throughout their organisation. In this book the focus was much more on the individual's personal change to a different, better way of working and whilst I could have included many more tools and techniques it was important to me that this ought to be the beginning rather than the end of the reader's learning journey. It needed to provide enough insight and motivation to get them started and to start winning, which would beget a hunger for more and drive an insatiable appetite to get better every day.

And so I left stuff out…

Where's Value Stream Mapping? What about 5S / workplace organisation? Surely we need more information on standardised work? And many other items from the Lean toolkit.

However, if you've read the book from the front cover to this point and you're still asking these questions, I've failed in the intent and purpose of the book, because it's about the emotional, BTFA cycle much more than the intellectual, PDCA cycle and it is intentional that you might need to read more and learn more about other Lean tools to become a real intellectual Lean thinker, but this book *should* provide you with everything that you need to live Lean in your everyday life. As I mentioned in Chapter 10, I don't expect and wouldn't advise that you follow my personal ways-of-working precisely, but if you don't live Lean you'll find that the problems that prompted you to read this book will continue to haunt your daily effectiveness. I promise you that what I left out will not be the cause of you not being successful in your personal change; only my failure to spark a BTFA change in you, or your change missing one of the VCRSP elements can do that.

Getting personal

Before I finish the penultimate chapter of the book, I'd like to provide you with a final personal example of how I live what I'm teaching in this book, a demonstration of 'walking the talk', if you will. At the same time that I set the objective of writing this book as part of my personal Hoshin for 2020, I also established two other objectives for the year. This was another example of the power of three and I find that three personal breakthrough objectives per year is a number that works well for me. The one that I want to use as my example was actually the first that I prioritised, that of losing weight.

Before getting into the details of this example, I'm going to explain why I won't provide any statistics in this story, as I worry that the use of data might actually get in the way of the message. For example, I'm going to talk to you about running and my participation in marathons and half-marathons, for which many readers will wonder what my PB (personal best) times are and, whilst I'm happy to tell you that I don't run Boston marathon qualifier times, I'm also not worried about being caught by the round-up stewards. Nevertheless, if I was to disclose my times in this example it might distract you from considering what the change process was that I went through and my emotional journey through BTFA, and you might instead focus on whether you run faster or slower than me. I therefore sought to take that risk out of the equation by omitting the data and talking in relative terms.

I'd been about the same weight, plus or minus, ever since I started recreational running, having made a lifestyle change around 10 years ago that made me feel a lot fitter and hit a weight at the top of my medically recommended range. However, for the last couple of years I'd felt frustrated that, despite having kept good gym attendance, eating pretty healthfully and running 3–4 times per week, I still couldn't get myself to my recommended BMI level.[2] I therefore decided that doing so should be a personal Hoshin objective for this year. I began 2020 with a focus on reducing my weight and set myself up with a measuring regime that saw me weigh myself once per week at the same time so that I could track my weight week-on-week (short-interval control), I continued my gym training and running regime, and I focussed on even healthier eating. Nevertheless, after two months, at the end of February, I had made no significant progress and what I determined was that I'd made the fatal mistake of repeating the same behaviour and expecting a different result! Therefore, at the beginning of March I did some problem solving and determined two key changes that I would make:

1. I would start following the 16–8 diet,[3] which is an intermittent fasting diet whereby you fast for 16 hours of the day and only eat during an 8-hour window. Whilst you cannot simply eat what you like during that 8-hour period, you can be less restrictive in your diet, as the key element is that your body has a 16-hour period in which it doesn't have to digest food. I therefore chose to fast between 20:00 (8 pm) and 12:00 (12 pm), which allowed me to maximise the part of it when I was sleeping!

2. I would stop running and focus on walking as my form of cardiovascular exercise. The reason for this was twofold. Firstly, I determined that running had significantly improved my stamina and cardiovascular fitness but that I'd 'hit a wall' in terms of weight loss, compensating for the higher level of calorie loss through higher calorie intake. Secondly, a lot of the time I need to do my exercise in the morning to fit it around my work and other commitments and, in combination with the 16–8 diet, that would mean running on an empty stomach and then not being able to eat until several hours after the run, which I felt was unsustainable.

This was a big change and stopping running really seemed counterintuitive, as exchanging running with walking, an exercise that would burn fewer calories per hour, didn't seem sensible. Nevertheless, this is something that I've also found in business, that to make a breakthrough change you must do things that are perhaps counterintuitive. I really did miss a few things, in particular my runs, which since starting have been almost therapeutic and during which I've conceived a lot of the content of the articles and books that I've written. I also missed the light but tasty breakfast that I used to have each morning, especially my glass of grapefruit juice. However, I soon got used to the routine and started to enjoy my lunch and dinner with a renewed appetite. Whilst progress wasn't straightforward, as I would sometimes have what I thought was a great week only to discover that my weight had only slightly reduced or not at all, ultimately I applied discipline and short-interval control to ensure that I stuck to it and, at the time of writing, I had successfully met my interim target and I am on track to hit the ultimate target level for this objective.

Please be careful as you think about my example. If you have some ideas about what I should have done differently or better, forget them. If you're struggling to lose weight and can't understand why this approach worked for me and not for you, please stop thinking about that. If you're thinking about *my problem*, you've missed the moral of my story, which is about setting objectives, putting in place all of the elements of VCRSP, applying daily management, short-interval control, problem solving, etc., and getting the result that you want. What *you* want to achieve. My story is my own; I want you to make your story one that you can successfully tell to others.

I hope that this chapter has added value for you, as I felt that it would be useful to give you some tangible examples of how *Living Lean* works for me and I decided to use examples related to personal rather than professional goals, as there are many of the latter already documented in my books and articles.

Finding what works for you, and experimenting new ways-of-working, is critical to *Living Lean* and I wish you much success as you continue on your personal transformation.

Hansei

Before moving onto the next chapter, please take a few moments to reflect and consider what, in relation to your own way of working and actions, are:

Your key learning points?

The changes that you could make?

Current problems that they would help to solve?

Notes

1 Thomas Jefferson, Steve Jobs, and the Rule of 3, Carmine Gallo, *Forbes*, 2nd July 2012. (www.forbes.com/sites/carminegallo/2012/07/02/thomas-jefferson-steve-jobs-and-the-rule-of-3/#51b3a6e71962)

2 BMI is Body Mass Index and is a medical measure of weight relative to height, which provides a range from underweight to recommended weight range, overweight range and obese. (www.nhs.uk/live-well/healthy-weight/bmi-calculator/)

3 The 16:8 intermittent fasting diet involves only eating during an 8-hour period during the day and has been associated with supporting a healthy weight loss and maintenance regime. (www.medicalnewstoday.com/articles/327398#side-effects-and-risks)

Chapter 12

Epilogue

The intention of this final chapter is to use a LinkedIn article[1] that I wrote in 2017 to emphasise the change in thinking that *Living Lean* requires. It confronts the subject of being too busy and proposes that it may well be that, if you are, you might not be doing it right...

If you're too busy, you're not doing it right

Many years ago I played squash for the first time. I was new to the company and town and was befriended by a colleague, Steve, who suggested that we play a game of squash at the local sports centre. What I didn't know at the time of accepting his offer was that he once played squash for Wales and that his son was currently Wales' number two player and so he possessed quite a lot of knowledge of, and skill in, the game. The game went as you might expect, ending after what seemed like a lifetime, me leaving the court drenched in sweat and squarely beaten. Steve on the other hand strolled off having hardly broken a sweat, having spent most of his time occupying the centre of the court as he sent a man 20 years his junior on what I will call a 'journey of learning' about the game of squash.

If you look at this in the context of performance it is clear that I was the busy one, working very hard and having little time to do anything other than to constantly chase the ball around the court in the vain attempt to win the point. Steve on the other hand was effective, using only the energy

DOI: 10.4324/9781003251385-16

needed and being competent enough, and in control, to win the game with ease. Certainly this is an extreme example as he was an experienced player and I was a novice and, had he been playing against a more evenly matched opponent, I'm certain that he would have had to expend much more effort and been suitably tired at the end of the game.

Nevertheless, whatever the sport might be, if you think about those players who are really good at the sport that they play, they typically do not behave in the way that amateurs do when they play the sport. They focus their energy, using their experience and knowledge to determine where it makes sense to stretch themselves, how to utilise their time and how they intend to win that next point, yard, or whatever the advantage is that they aim to win. They are busy but they're not too busy to give themselves the opportunity to succeed. Contrast this with many people in business, who are consistently too busy to be on time, to pay attention in meetings, to answer emails or to meet deadlines. 'I'm just too busy' sometimes seems like it has become a valid excuse not to deliver on commitments or, even more worryingly, has become a 'badge of honour' for some.

There are myriad causes for the overload of people, and I don't wish to blame individuals, as many organisations have created a culture of overload of their staff and the consequent disengagement of the vast majority of their employees. Nevertheless, I do make a plea to individuals to take the responsibility to solve the problem for yourselves and your teams, taking some simple steps to improve the situation. These steps are simple but they are not necessarily easy to implement, as they do require a change in behaviour, which in some cases is potentially counterintuitive. Some of the improvement approaches are as follows:

Hoshin Kanri

One of the biggest issues that most organisations face is initiative overload. I often joke that most companies are like a child in a sweet shop (candy store), with so much to choose from that they cannot choose and they finally eat too much and become ill. This means that they take on too many projects and fail to complete them on time and to the right quality level, with disparate objectives across teams and the overloading and potential burn-out of their people.

The implementation of Hoshin Kanri (policy deployment) is the most effective way to ensure that the organisation doesn't 'bite off more than it can chew' and that its people are aligned toward delivering the same objectives. This involves learning how to say the 'intelligent no', not accepting some requests but with an intelligent explanation as to why and how the requestor's needs might be met in a different way. Whilst this is something best implemented at the organisational level, it doesn't prevent individual teams from garnering benefit from its implementation as, whilst they will find alignment issues where other teams are not utilising Hoshin Kanri, the way that they deal with this will still be significantly better than they were doing previously. They will also be able to act as a role model of Hoshin Kanri and help to persuade other teams, and ultimately the whole organisation, to adopt this way of working.

Daily management

Many teams simply don't know how they are performing in a short enough interval to make an adjustment before they fail. Often performance reviews are geared around explaining why the team failed, looking at 'lagging indicators' that tell them how they performed last week, last month or last quarter. Sometimes it can feel like it is simply an inquest into the failure to meet targets and a very defensive discussion. This is a little like trying to drive a car by looking in the rear view mirror, certain to provide a view of what has been but soon resulting in a crash of some form. Contrast this with those teams that undertake daily management, determining the 'leading indicators' that will allow them to determine if they are on the right track and reviewing them on a short interval. Those teams truly own their performance as they can quickly predict when performance is drifting, rapidly problem solving to ensure that they 'course correct' before their customers know that they're off-course.

Competence management

Whilst it might be unfashionable to say as much, a lot of employees are incompetent in their roles. This is not to say that they are not skilled or educated but that they have not been adequately trained to do the job in question. It is not uncommon for team members to be thrown straight into a role without any formal training, simply assuming that, because they are qualified for the job, they know what to do. This is disingenuous and the cause of much ineffectiveness in the workplace. It is exacerbated by the 'Dunning–Kruger' effect, where the less experienced person vastly overestimates their competence level. This is what might be colloquially termed as 'a little knowledge is dangerous'. An organisation must therefore ensure that it has a competence management system in place and operating effectively if it is to achieve a highly competent workforce.

Whilst the organisation must implement an effective competence management system, the individual must open their self to learning, being conscious of the Dunning–Kruger effect and being humble enough to admit and accept that being qualified for a role does not equate to being immediately competent for the role. Conscious incompetence (knowing what you don't know) is a skill that we all must master if we are to be true learners and therefore an individual should spend significant time to understand the concept and develop their willingness to admit the status.

Be the culture

Accepting defeat to the current culture is unacceptable if we are to make change and so every individual employee must pledge to be the culture that they want and not assume the culture that exists. The best way that I've found to express this is:

> ...if I simply sit, passively, waiting for a culture change program to be launched, or for senior management to change the culture, then I am simultaneously the victim and the perpetrator of this 'crime against high performance'.

The responsibility of the individual is therefore to act in a way that models what they want the culture to be, rather than what they believe that it currently dictates.

Problem solving

The problem-solving skills of most team members are weak and must be developed to a much higher level if we are to achieve excellence. Far too often conclusions are jumped to due to the sheer weight of time pressure and the normal human instinct to jump to a conclusion. Furthermore, many problems are escalated quickly to a high level, overwhelming the leadership and ensuring that there are more problems than could possibly be resolved. It is therefore imperative that the team members are taught how to problem solve effectively and that they are empowered and expected to solve the majority of problems without escalation. It takes time and effort to develop the skill but, as it is perfected, it will result in a significant amount of freed-up time at the more senior levels.

Time management

The most important element of time management to understand is that multi-tasking is ineffective. Those people who believe that they are great multi-taskers are, in fact, simply fast switchers between tasks but have been proven time and again to be less effective than those people who focus on one task at a time. Getting your time management right is critical to success, as time cannot be caught up or replaced; once it is spent, it is spent. Therefore, how we spend our time is a much more significant decision than the majority of us choose to make it.

If you are prepared to change your ways of working as described above, you will ultimately be more successful individually and will be able to influence better performance for your organisation. It is natural and easy to fall into the trap of overload, and being over-busy, but you do need to decide, metaphorically speaking, how you wish to play squash, and to keep in mind that:

If you're too busy, you're not doing it right

Hansei

Before completing the book, please take a few moments to reflect and consider what, in relation to your own way of working and actions, are:

Your key learning points?

The changes that you could make?

Current problems that they would help to solve?

Note

1 If You're Too Busy, You're Not Doing It Right, Philip Holt, LinkedIn, 9th May 2017. (www.linkedin.com/pulse/youre-too-busy-doing-right-philip-holt/)

Index

Printed in the United States
by Baker & Taylor Publisher Services